FINDING FISH

Finding Fish

LOCATING AND CATCHING FISH

IN WARM-WATER LAKES

Cliff Hauptman

 Lyons & Burford, Publishers

Printed in the United States of America

10 9 8 7 6 5 4 3 2 1

Library of Congress Cataloging-in-Publication Data

Hauptman, Cliff.
    Finding fish : locating and catching fish in warm-water lakes / Cliff Hauptman.
        p.   cm.
    Includes bibliographical references and index.
    ISBN 1-55821-160-8
    √1. Fishing.   2. Freshwater fishes. √ I. Title.
SH441.H343   1992
799.1'2—dc20   92-7299
                                                            CIP

To SUSIE who doesn't fish

and to MOLLY who one day might.

Contents

"*Man*: Is this a game of chance?
"*W. C. Fields*: (shuffling the cards): Not the way *I* play. No."

—My Little Chicadee

FINDING FISH

Introduction

TO HAVE A CLUE

Although there may be plenty of other reasons to go fishing, the ultimate goal of most anglers is to catch fish. That can only be accomplished with regularity if you are fishing where the fish are. So if the ultimate goal is to *catch* fish, the initial goal must be to *find* them.

Inexperienced anglers all too often believe that if they plunk their bait or lure in the water and no fish hits it, then the fish are simply not biting. "The fish weren't biting" is a common grievance among anglers who do not realize that the fish have to be found before they can be caught.

Finding fish requires a plan. Fishing without a plan is nothing more than tossing dice. Because fish are not scattered evenly throughout a lake, all waiting

eagerly for an angler to drop them a line, your proba-
bility of choosing a productive spot by mere luck is very
small—about one in ten. If you approach each fishing
outing with a plan of attack, however, you can increase
your likelihood of finding and catching fish to a near
certainty. That's quite a difference.

To formulate a decent plan, you need to know the
clues that are being provided by the lake and the fish
that live in it. This book will show you where to find
those clues and how to put them all together to reach a
conclusion and devise a plan. The purpose of the plan
will be to locate fish; catching them will be largely up
to you, although this book will provide a few tips on
that, too.

Having a plan is essential to successful fishing, and
I define successful fishing as being able to go out any-
time, on nearly any body of water, and catch fish on a
reasonably consistent basis. The plan must vary according to your analysis of several shifting factors that
affect fishing. Some of those factors—time of day,
weather conditions, and season, for example—are easy
to determine, but their significance may not be apparent. Others, like the types of cover and structure on the
lake bottom, may have a clearer significance but be
harder to determine. Still others, like the proper lures
to use once you've examined the other factors, may
have to come from intuition gained through experience. In any case, the angler who chooses to regard
fishing as a system of random successes is going to
meet with very few, while the one with a strategy will
most often prevail.

But a plan has to be based on accurate knowledge
and insight in order to work. The key is to realize a few
things that most anglers apparently do not:

- Practically every warm-water lake has some fishable species in it. Whether a water hazard on a golf course, a farm or neighborhood pond of only a few acres, a natural or man-made lake with significant shoreline development, a reservoir, or a large natural lake or impoundment untouched by humans, there are fish in residence. This comes as a great shock to nonanglers, and even anglers fail to recognize this fact, but fact it is nonetheless.
- Fish are not machines; they are natural organisms like flowers and birds. Part of this problem with the perception of fish is that fish are not readily observable to most people. Even non-botanists and non-ornithologists are aware of the seasonal changes in the behaviors of plants and birds because people who take particular interest in plants and birds can watch them and observe their complex and subtle interactions with the rest of the world on an ongoing basis. People, whether angler or nonangler, who are interested in fish cannot readily do that, which makes it easy to ignore that fish, too, are complex and subtle organisms.
- Fish are not all over a lake. Large percentages of any lake are unsuitable as fish habitat. Most of these areas lack sufficient food, protection from enemies, comfortable temperatures or levels of dissolved oxygen, or any number of requirements. In any case, no amount of persistence will help you catch fish in a section of water in which fish do not care to reside.
- Every fish in a lake has a specific reason for being where it is at any particular time. Fish do not wander around aimlessly and settle down randomly.
- Fish interrelate with their environment. The char-

acteristics of the body of water in which a fish lives determine that interrelationship. Fish relate variously with the plant growth, depth, and bottom topography of a lake depending on a multitude of changing factors that include time of day, time of year, weather, and even boat traffic.

- Different species of fish have behaviors that are unlike the behaviors of other species and that influence where, how, and when we can best fish for them, even within a single lake.
- The most effective way to catch individual fish in a given lake can change from minute to minute, often from hour to hour, usually from day to day, and most assuredly from month to month.
- Successful fishing can often be simple, but it is never mindless. The outward simplicity of fishing as a sport—the relative ease with which the use of its equipment can be mastered, the lack of a need for athletic prowess, its universal availability—is deceptive. Certainly, anyone can stick some bait on a hook and sling it into the water; he will also catch fish on occasion. Likewise, anyone can pick up a phone, dial a broker, and invest in a randomly selected stock; he may be lucky enough to make a buck as well. But in neither case will the participant consistently meet with success because he is operating on luck only. In both cases, a solid background and understanding of the subject will significantly shift the balance between skill and luck.
- Nothing anyone says about fishing is gospel. Because we are working with living creatures in a larger system that we imperfectly understand, fishing remains an imprecise science. That is why, thank god, the definitive book about fishing has not

yet been, and never will be, written. That is also why fishing will remain a lifelong passion for so many people; the more you know about it, the more interesting it becomes.

To the insufficiently enlightened, fishing is a passive activity—the act of casting notwithstanding—in which the angler waits to be visited by good fortune. To fishermen who know what they are doing, however, fishing is a continually demanding series of problem-solving situations in which so many loose ends are held in the lips at once that success is felt not only in the physical and emotional charge of a fighting creature at the end of the line, but as a concrete intellectual triumph as well.

That kind of problem-solving reduces luck to second-rate status, for, nine times out of ten, an angler who catches a fish is merely lucky, but an angler who, during that same outing, can consistently duplicate that success because he understands the mechanisms involved is a good fisherman. Make no mistake, luck will always be a welcome partner to the astute fisherman, but it is not his only partner.

For me, one of the greatest joys of fishing is the kick I get from its irony: Fishing allows a serious angler to entirely clear his mind of interfering matters of consequence so that he may focus all his concentration, all his physical, mental, and emotional energies on a problem whose ultimate solution has no importance whatsoever.

That said, herein is the wherewithal for going out onto the surface of a warm-water lake, familiar or unknown, and having at least a clue how to enjoy successful fishing.

1

Warm-Water Lakes

THE GENERAL ENVIRONMENT

A warm-water lake is one in which species of warm-water fish—largemouth bass, bluegill, sunfish, pickerel, crappie, yellow perch, and others of that ilk—naturally reside, overwinter, spawn, and thrive. That is, as opposed to a cold-water lake more suited to trout and in which most of the warm-water species will not thrive.

That definition is technically correct, but it requires a fair amount of embellishment to make it useful. Where, for example, do the terms regarding the water temperature fit? Clearly, an ice fisherman who is catching largemouth bass in New England in January has a reasonable argument when he asserts that the lake he is fishing is full of cold water. To understand the apparent contradiction, you must briefly stray into

the area of lake ecology, which is actually a branch—
or, perhaps, just a twig—of geology.

Natural lakes go through an aging and maturing
process that changes their characteristics over a vast
period of time. Ironically, though, time is not the factor
by which the age of lakes is determined, for lakes that
are *geologically* older may be *ecologically* younger.
Rather, the factor by which natural lakes are compared
involves, at its most basic, the rate at which usable
food is produced and stored through photosynthesis.
That sounds like the kind of thing only an aquatic biologist can determine through clinical analysis of water
samples, but it luckily manifests itself in such ways
that become obvious to the lay observer.

Ecologically young lakes are said to be *oligotrophic*.
They produce very little food, having a low level of nutrients in proportion to the amount of water. Such
lakes are usually deep, clear, rocky, and scantily
weeded. Their sides are steep with very little area in
which sediments can settle and plants can take root.
The water in these lakes does not stratify into different
temperature and oxygen layers. Dissolved oxygen is
equally distributed throughout the lake, even to its
deepest parts, allowing fish to inhabit all of the water
throughout the year. Oligotrophic lakes are the norm
in the Canadian Shield and northern New England.
They provide the ideal habitat for lake trout but little
else. Their waters are cold even in summer. Their food
chains have very few links. The tendency of such a lake
is toward *eutrophication*. That is to say that over
time—the amount of which varies according to several
ancillary factors—a natural lake tends to collect nutrients through the buildup of sediments that will grade

its shorelines more gently, thereby offering larger areas for plants to root, for more sediments to accumulate, for more living things to thrive and die and add to the nutrient and sediment base.

Eventually a natural lake reaches old age and is said to be *eutrophic*. Its water is rich in nutrients and weed growth covers all but the deepest hole, which may be no deeper than thirty feet. Structurally, eutrophic lakes are characteristically muck-bottomed and shallow. Average depth is most often less than twenty feet, with most of the water occurring over shallow weed-covered flats from two to ten feet in depth. Surface weeds such as lily pads often blanket the shallows. Some of these lakes may have sunken islands and underwater humps with weed growth on their tops. The water is usually stained or murky, and dissolved oxygen is scarce in the depths. Water temperatures throughout the lake can reach as high as air temperatures in the summer months.

In the latest, extreme stages of eutrophication, a lake loses its ability to support fish. Just prior to that stage, only fish that are able to survive in soupy waters with very low levels of dissolved oxygen remain— primitive bowfins (mudfish in Florida), bullheads (hornpout in some areas), and carp. After those go, the lake is on its way to becoming dry land.

In between the pure oligotrophic and pure eutrophic stages is a condition with a great deal of range and variation. And, of course, it is somewhere within that wide swath that most of the natural lakes in the United States fall.

At some point, moving from oligotrophic toward eutrophic, a lake becomes suitable not only for lake trout but for walleye, smallmouth bass, and northern pike. Its sides become more gradual, filled with rock rubble and some plant growth and thus creating suitable spawning areas and safe havens for a variety of species. Eventually, the lake's characteristics change to the point where its water stratifies into separate temperature and oxygen layers. There is a large area at the bottom, below the *thermocline* (the layer of quickly changing temperature that separates the warmer upper layer from the colder bottom layer), where there is almost no dissolved oxygen. The lake's suitability for lake trout lapses, and other cool-water species predominate. Such *mesotrophic* lakes abound in a narrow band that extends across the northern part of the United States and includes, roughly, southern New England, New York, the states that touch the southern Great Lakes, and those of the northern plains.

As a lake's progress toward eutrophication continues and its bottom supports more and more weed growth on shallow points and flats, largemouth bass and a variety of warm-water panfish will find it a suitable habitat, and both the cool-water and warm-water species will share the lake in a shifting balance of dominance until the lake is no longer habitable by the cool-water species. It then becomes a purely warm-water lake. That progression may take tens of thousands of years, and it rarely goes smoothly and perfectly. The result is that there are thousands of lakes today, somewhere along the process of eutrophication, that have sections within them at different stages. A large lake may be relatively rocky and barren at one end and weedy and shallow at the other. Such lakes tend to hold a happy variety of species for the sportsman.

Manmade impoundments, too, can be particularly abundant in unnaturally occurring varieties of cold-, cool-, and warm-water species precisely because they are not naturally formed. The intentional flooding of particular terrains creates situations in which underwater habitats that would never have occurred through the natural process of eutrophication are adjoined to form super-habitats for fish and other aquatic species.

The Model Warm-Water Lake

The warm-water lakes of this book's title exist in abundance throughout the country. They are the lakes most fished by the vast majority of anglers pursuing the nation's most popular gamefish, the largemouth bass, and the nation's most popular panfish, the bluegill. They also harbor a challenging variety of other panfish and gamefish.

Yet, there are no two lakes exactly alike, even if they share a precise stage of eutrophication. Every warm-water lake is unique and presents its own specific problems to the angler. Fortunately, though, most warm-water lakes do share at least a few of several characteristics that can be discussed in terms both general and specific, and that allow me to teach you to read a warm-water lake without having to analyze every single body of water between Boston and San Diego. To that end, it will be helpful to create an idealized warm-water lake, one that has several of the important features, so that you can transfer your grasp of those features to other lakes that share them.

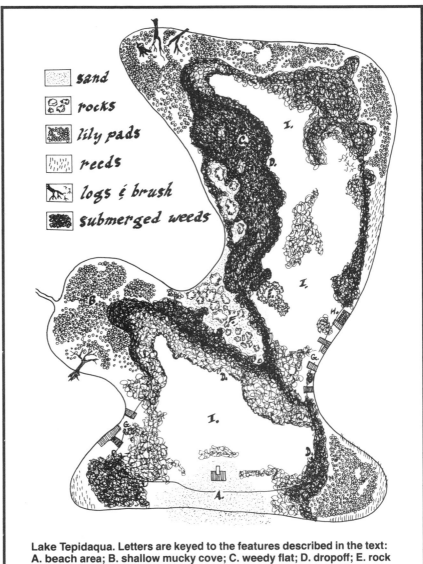

**Lake Tepidaqua. Letters are keyed to the features described in the text:
A. beach area; B. shallow mucky cove; C. weedy flat; D. dropoff; E. rock
pile; F. point; G. docks; H. shoreline dropoff; I. deeper open water.**

The size of a lake does not matter much, except in its carrying capacity and in the time it may take you to explore and get to know it. Small lakes of around fifty to three hundred acres are my favorites because of their manageable size, but I often seek out much smaller ponds of areas between five and fifty acres. Particularly large lakes usually can be thought of as several smaller lakes joined together. In any case, being warm-water lakes, they will share some of the following traits.

A small private-beach area with a diving raft often exhibits the same general conditions as . . .

. . . a large public-swimming area with rafts and marked boundaries.

Most warm-water lakes have several coves of this type, ranging in size from cozy nooks that can be covered in a few casts to acres of lilypad-covered expanses.

Beach Area This need not be an actual formal beach, but many natural warm-water lakes have an area of shoreline from which a sandy bottom gradually slopes down to deep water. In the case of an actual beach, either private or public, weeds are most often cleared from the shallows, but appear in clumps along the edges of the designated area or are allowed to grow as the water gets deep. The important characteristic is a sand bottom that gradually deepens to about fifteen feet or more.

Shallow Mucky Cove This is an area that, in the peak of summer, is nearly inaccessible even by boat. A dense carpet of lily pads covers most of the cove, which is only a foot deep at its innermost end and deepens to about four feet at the outer edge of the pads. The bottom is black muck, composed of the rotting vegetation that has been collecting for years. Beyond the edge of the pads, a thick bed of subsurface weeds grows about three feet tall from the bottom as the water gradually deepens to about seven feet. A small inlet stream feeds the lake at the back of this cove.

Weedy Flat Here is an area of nearly uniform depth. Closest to the shore, the bottom quickly grades to about three feet deep and very gradually deepens to only about ten feet at its outer edge. The average depth over most of the flat is five feet, with a variety of weeds covering its entire area. Its bottom is soft but not mucky. A flat may be a relatively narrow strip along the shoreline, or it may be an expanse of several acres extending dozens of yards into the lake. The outer edge of a flat is typically defined by a dropoff.

Dropoff The dropoff usually defines the outer edges of several areas. Here, for instance, it sharply de-

A level weedy flat extends from the near edge of the surface weeds all the way to the foreground of the photo. The bottom is about four feet deep.

This flat is about eight feet deep and extends under all the water you can see in the photo.

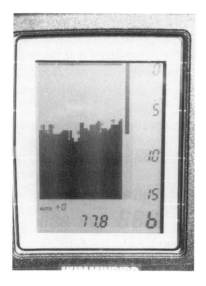

On a liquid crystal sonar screen, the eight-foot flat shows the weeds to be growing to within six feet of the surface. The surface temperature of the water is 77.8 degrees Fahrenheit.

This sonar display shows a steep dropoff from seven feet down to fifteen and then some.

fines the outer edge of the flat, dropping off from ten feet to fifteen or more, as if off the edge of a wall; weed growth stops abruptly at the lip. Where it meets the mucky cove, however, it is not as sharp, nor is it as sudden at the ends of the flat. There the dropoff is a bit more gradual, allowing more weed growth along its slope.

Rockpile This may be an island that does not quite make it to the surface, or it may actually be a pile of rocks that glacial action has left, fortuitously, in some deeper part of the lake. In manmade impoundments, it may be the remains of a raised roadbed on the bottom of the lake. In any case, it may vary in size from the kind of heap left by a couple of dump trucks full of stones to an acre or more in area. Some humps are

Emergent weed growth indicates the presence of a rock pile that comes nearly to the surface out of about ten feet of water.

Many rock piles do not come near the surface. This sonar display shows one side of a broad rock pile that rises to within ten feet of the surface from a seventeen-foot bottom.

weed-covered and some are bare. Some are steep-sided, falling away to deep water, and some provide a gradual slope along their sides. Still others are steep-sided on one side and sloped gradually on the other.

Point   A rock pile or submerged hump that is attached to the shore at one end is a point. Usually, these are underwater continuations of shoreline points and ridges that run right into the lake. Most are gradually tapering, both horizontally and vertically. Some are soft-bottomed and are covered with weeds until they reach a depth, at which the weeds slack off. Others are rocky, containing little or no weed growth. Points may also be steep-sided, dropping quickly off into deep water along their sides.

Large points that extend far into a lake usually continue under water to form important structure that attracts fish of many species.

The presence of houses on a point usually indicates that the point drops off quickly into deep water.

Docks Populated lakes, which are certainly the majority whether for summer cottages or year-round residences, usually have some docks or boathouses along their shorelines. Some of these will be solely for the launching and docking of small boats, in which case they may be in shallow water. Others will be for swimming and diving or for the docking of larger boats. These latter docks will most often extend into deeper water.

Shoreline Dropoff This is a dropoff to deep water quite close to shore. Unlike the beach area, the point, the cove, or the flat, here there is little shallow-water area between the shore and deep water. Such a place may be the site of a rope swing from which swimmers safely dive into deep water. The shortage of shallows here precludes much weed growth, although reeds may populate the narrow strip near shore.

Deeper, Open Water This is the deepest open-water part of the lake beyond the dropoffs. Depending on its depth and the clarity of the water, it may support weed growth on its mucky bottom or not. Sometimes its shape reflects that of the shoreline; it may actually be "out in the middle," but is often at one end of a lake.

Each of these common features is indicated on the accompanying illustration of an idealized warm-water lake that I will call "Lake Tepidaqua." There are thousands of lakes remarkably similar to this model, and tens of thousands that share at least a few of its features. What you learn about how fish relate to the features of Lake Tepidaqua will apply to similar features in other warm-water lakes.

First, though, a more detailed look at those features.

This large house has not only a spacious boathouse, but an expansive dock/deck that extends far over the water.

The steep slope of the land on this shoreline indicates a nearly immediate drop into deep water. Often there is a narrow shallow shelf before the dropoff, a favorite nesting area for bluegills.

The near foreground of this photo is just about at the edge of a dropoff to deep water of about twenty feet. The deep open water extends to within about one hundred feet of the far shore, where the bottom suddenly rises onto an eight-foot-deep weedy flat that gradually grades to shore.

2

Cover, Structure, and Edges

THE SPECIFIC ENVIRONMENT

What is Cover?

Assuming that a lake can provide a fish with the basics necessary to sustain its life—water that does not reach lethal temperatures, food, and dissolved oxygen—the next most important attribute is cover. Cover, basically, is anything in a fish's environment that offers a place to hide.

Cover is most apparently necessary to prey species as a place to find safety from predators. But it is equally essential to predators as a place from which to ambush prey. Clearly then, good cover is a place around which most of a fish's activity takes place; either the fish is hiding from something or waiting to grab something—usually both: It's a jungle out there.

But cover does not have to relate to food. As you will learn in the next chapter, light plays an important role in the behavior of fish, and cover provides a fish with the means of mitigating the effects of ultraviolet light on its comfort. The availability of the right type of cover is also critical to a fish's choice of spawning area.

Most cover is provided by weeds, wood, rocks, the shoreline, and manmade objects.

WEEDS

Weeds are the primary cover in any warm-water lake. Like vegetation on dry land, aquatic plants provide the foundation of the food chain in a lake. Aquatic insects, snails, crayfish, and some minnows feed directly on plants. Those creatures, as well as the young of our quarry, in turn provide the forage for the fish we anglers are trying to catch.

Weeds also provide excellent protection for young fish, which are attracted to weeds in order to escape larger fish, which are in turn attracted to weeds in search of those smaller fish that are hiding from them. The principal gamefish of warm-water lakes—bass and pickerel—are predators that rely on ambush. They tend to lie motionless among weeds and rush out at passing prey. Even a perfunctory look at the markings on the flanks of bass and pickerel will reveal how excellently they will be concealed among weeds in dappled underwater light.

Weeds also produce oxygen through photosynthesis. That means, of course, that weedy areas tend to be better oxygenated than areas barren of weeds, and fish need dissolved oxygen to thrive. The oxygen situation, though, is not so cut and dried, for an especially weedy area may actually use up all the oxygen it produces in the decomposition of its own waste materials. That may be particularly true in very shallow areas where the water gets exceedingly warm (the ability of water to hold oxygen decreases as the water warms) and where the water is especially murky. Compared to such a spot, a rocky point over which the wind action constantly mixes the water with air will be better oxygenated.

Weeds with floating leaves provide both cover from overhead dangers—ospreys, kingfishers, wading birds, raccoons, anglers—and shade. They are also rich in food, for frogs, dragonflies, snakes, and other creatures congregate on and among floating leaves. Most com-

Weeds with floating leaves, like these water lilies, are often the most apparent forms of cover on a lake.

Filamentous weeds also form floating mats.

monly, plants with floating leaves are referred to generically as lily pads, and I will follow suit. But it can be useful at times to know that plants with floating leaves include a variety of species of water lilies, spatterdock, frogbits, water shield, floatinghearts, and a few other plants, all of which are characterized by having roundish, floating leaves that tend to form patches of cover. In the South, water lettuce and water hyacinth also provide floating cover.

Filamentous surface weeds also provide overhead cover, food, oxygen, and points of ambush. Bladderwort, for example, is a free-floating plant without visible roots that tends to form large mats on the surface of a lake. Other plants, like coontail and hydrilla, may be rooted in the bottom but grow to such lengths that their tops lie upon the water in floating mats.

Filamentous weeds can play havoc with lures, even those designed to be weedless.

Emergent weeds are another important source of cover. Such plants include reeds, cattails, grasses, pickerelweeds, and any other kinds of plants that are rooted underwater but stick straight up out of the water, inevitably in the extreme shallows. Such plants do not appear to offer much cover, nor does the water seem deep enough to hold fish, yet large gamefish— mainly bass, pickerel, and pike—are regularly caught in less than a foot of water and lying in ambush within skinny vegetation of just this type.

Often more important to anglers, though, are the subsurface beds of weeds that are not easily seen. Much

These arrowheads are an example of emergent weeds that include pickerelweed, cattails, and other leafy and reedy plants that like to keep their feet wet.

of the bottom of a warm-water lake is covered with a variety of plant species that form a lush garden upon the flats, humps, points, and slopes under water. Some of those species, like watermilfoil and various Cabomba, have dense, feathery leaves, while others, like the pondweeds, have broad cabbagy foliage. Each species grows in its preferred habitat, forming lush stands of dense cover at various depths, and it is in these that most of the fish are to be found during much of the summer.

All aquatic plants, then, are key to finding fish because of their vital role as cover.

Coontail is an example of a submerged weed that forms dense beds under water. Occasionally, coontail grows so tall that its tips poke through the surface.

Fallen trees are common along the shores of most warm-water lakes and provide important cover.

Logs may be entirely submerged, in which case you must look carefully to locate them.

WOOD

In natural lakes, fallen trees provide a limited amount of cover. When an old dead oak, its branches long gone to storms and insects, finally loses hold of the bank and falls in the water, it begins a new life as cover for fish. Still holding some nutrients on which life can thrive, the massive log will play host to gardens of algae. Snails, insects, and minnows will be attracted to that source of food, and larger predators will move in. The log provides shade and food, and is important cover.

When an otherwise healthy pine is uprooted by a storm and falls into a lake, its fully branched and needled crown provides more substantial cover, contributing that much more surface area for plant growth and a much more intricate network of hidey-holes for protection and ambush.

In manmade impoundments, where flooded groves of standing timber are typical, the significance of wood as cover becomes critical, often rivaling weeds as the most important cover in an area.

In all warm-water lakes, submerged wood, whether in the form of fallen logs, fallen trees, brush, standing timber, or stumps, are extremely valuable cover.

ROCKS

It is amazing how many cracks, crevices, and crannies rocks can provide as cover. An ecologically young warm-water lake I once fished in Maine was entirely rock-strewn in one of its coves. The water was clear and shallow, and there was not a fish to be seen. There also

Rocks, like weeds and wood, may be emergent and obvious or entirely under water and obscure. In either case, they can provide both cover and structure.

seemed to be no place for fish to hide, so tightly packed were the boulders and slabs upon the bottom. Yet my casts into that cove produced more smallmouth bass than I ever imagined could survive in such a place. They came out from beneath, between, and behind every bit of boulder. It taught me an important lesson about rocks.

Not all eutrophic lakes have rocks, but most of the younger warm-water lakes, especially in the North, and many impoundments have rocky areas. Reservoirs often have riprap near their spillways, and manmade lakes and canals usually contain rock rubble from their construction.

Rocks, although not nearly as important as weeds in warm-water lakes, make good cover. Prey creatures, like crayfish and insect larvae, live among them, thereby attracting fish in search of food. They also tend to hold and release heat at a different rate from the water and vegetation around them, making them additionally important at certain times of the year, of which more later.

THE SHORELINE

The shoreline itself can provide cover in the form of undercut banks, submerged roots from lakeside trees, and overhanging foliage. These furnish shade, protection from predators, ambush points, food in the form of creatures that crawl off the bank or fall out of trees, and areas of more comfortable temperatures during parts of the fishes' yearly cycle.

The overhanging trees and bushes along this bank provide excellent cover. Their proximity to the lily pads makes this spot especially auspicious.

MANMADE OBJECTS

Docks, boathouses, and diving platforms or rafts provide cover similar to that offered by floating weeds and overhanging vegetation. Although not food magnets like the weeds, these structures do afford shade and a dark place from which a predator can ambush passersby.

The difficulty in locating productive cover is, of course, its relative invisibility. Surface weeds and docks are easy to spot and often provide good fishing, but when it is the underwater cover you should be prospecting, finding it can be a problem. A sonar unit is valuable, a pair of polarized sunglasses is a must, and the ability to make use of the evidence that comes back to you on your lures and anchor are indispensable. On an unfamiliar lake, it also always pays to ask the locals.

What is Structure?

Structure is simply a feature in the lake to which a fish can relate in terms of territory or orientation. A good way to think about structure is to imagine yourself crossing the vast empty prairies of Kansas and Nebraska in a covered wagon, trying to decide where to stop and build a house. You will absolutely seek out some feature in the landscape that is different from the rest. A river bend would be an obvious choice, a grove of cottonwoods another. Lacking anything conspicuous, you will look for a knoll or gully. Barring that, a barely noticeable rise or depression. In short, you will not

Diving platforms are usually located over deep water.

Boathouses provide shade in weedless and otherwise unshaded shallows.

simply plunk down any old place; you will naturally seek some identifiable feature, no matter how subtle, to which you can relate. And there you will build your home.

Fish tend to do the same thing. Certainly they seek the most abundant feeding areas, as well as the most expedient cover, but, given the option, they will occupy those areas of food and cover nearest to choice structure.

There are two manifestations of this behavior: solitary fish and schooling fish. Most mature gamefish tend to be effectively solitary. That is to say that even if a fish tends to remain in loose groups after the cohesive juvenile school breaks up, as is the case with bass, the large mature individuals are inclined toward giving themselves plenty of elbow room. Thus, the dominant bass in a given area will aggressively hold the best piece of structure in the best area of cover.

Schooling fish, like bluegills, perch, and crappies, will collectively relate to a piece of structure, the entire school orienting its activities around that particular feature.

In both cases, there is always more than one piece of structure involved. Both individuals and schools move about, as you will see, according to a variety of stimuli, and will relate to a variety of structural features at various times. They will also tend to follow structurally influenced routes during those movements.

This behavior of relating to specific objects is common in nature across a broad spectrum of animal types. You have undoubtedly seen a cloud of midges hanging nearly stationary in a patch of sunlight. The swarm is relating to some piece of structure in its environment, often a clump of grass, a stump, or the patch of light itself, and is using it as a marker to keep the mating swarm together. Dogs and cats choose very specific tufts of grass, logs, and other bits of "structure" on which to consistently leave their scents. Humans, as I have already indicated, are no different.

Structure in a warm-water lake may be either natural or manmade.

BOTTOM FEATURES

Any irregularities on a lake's bottom may be used by fish as a marker or point of reference. A rock amid weed beds, a stump or flooded bush, or a natural

This sonar display shows a 3½-foot-high rock or brush pile in thirteen feet of water. Notice the dots all around it. Those are fish attracted to this irregular bottom feature.

This sonar display indicates a three-foot stump in twelve feet of water. Again, fish are relating to it.

Here we see a gradual underwater slope on which weed growth suddenly stops about halfway down. That is an important structural feature to which fish relate.

depression are examples of structure commonly attractive to fish. But significant structure can be more subtle; the lips of flats are rarely straight-edged. More often, the dropoff cuts in and out, forming points and coves on the under-water flat. Such features are important structure, as are ridges, humps, and rock piles. If these features are large enough, prominent irregularities within them serve as structure, as well. In man-made impoundments, flooded road beds, old creek channels, and flooded standing timber are all important structure.

COVER AS STRUCTURE

Structure can also be cover, in which case it is particularly appealing to fish. If the outside edge of a

This stump among lily pads is an important structural feature as well as excellent cover.

The submerged leaves and branches of this leaning birch not only provide cover for small fish, but can act as a structural feature to which larger fish can relate.

bountiful weed bed is irregularly lobed so that fingers of the bed jut out and indentations cut in, fish will relate to those extremities as structure. Fish will also relate to isolated clumps of taller weeds amid a shorter bed. Fallen trees fully or partially submerged are prime cover as well as important structure.

MANMADE STRUCTURE

Old fishing cartoons used to make great sport of the angler who hoisted in an old tire, yet as odious as such pollution is, some manmade objects provide fish with structure to which they happily relate. Old quarries are traditional repositories for junked cars, and the fishing in such pits can be phenomenal as a result of

While these docks provide shady cover, their pilings act as structure.

the cover and structure those rusting hulks provide. More conventional, though, is the structure provided by wood or concrete bridge abutments, dock pilings, old Christmas trees that are commonly sunk to provide fish-attracting structure, and any flooded buildings, walls, or fences in impoundments.

As with cover, structure can be difficult to locate. Standing flooded timber, emergent rock piles, bridges, and an old road or wall that runs right down into an impoundment are real gifts. But most is invisible to the casual observer. A good sonar unit is highly advantageous for discerning bottom structure like the edges of dropoffs, underwater humps, and any subtle bottom irregularities to which fish may be attracted. A good unit will even depict outstanding growths of weeds and

The concrete abutments of this small bridge serve as structure. Larger
bridges can provide significant structure in their multiple abutments and
pilings.

This submerged fence acts as structure. In large impoundments, submerged fences, walls, roads, and even whole buildings are not uncommon.

variations in bottom texture. Besides electronics, polarized glasses will tremendously increase your ability to see below the surface. Bottom contour maps of a natural lake, although usually not detailed enough to indicate subtle variations in subsurface topography, will at least show the steepness and shape of points, dropoffs, and humps. Preflooding topo maps of impoundments are invaluable. And again, ask the locals.

A Little Edge Theory

The vast majority of creatures in any particular environment will be found around its edges. Take a small woodland as an example. Well within its interior you will find birds, insects, small mammals, a few snakes, a paucity of plant varieties and, perhaps, a deer or two if you are lucky. But where the woodland borders an open field, there you will find an enormous variety of plants, which in turn allows a greater variety of small mammals that eat those plants, and a resultant increase in snakes that eat small mammals. Likewise, the added variety of insect species that eat those plants attracts a larger number of bird species. The numbers of larger mammals also swells. The woodland provides haven for the animals while the meadow provides greater food and nesting opportunities. The edge at which the two environments meet contributes more to the whole than either of the environments alone. A grassy glen or pond in the midst of a woodland would offer the same efficacious edges.

A lake environment is subject to those same laws of nature. While a vast homogeneous bed of, say, coontail,

The front edge of this patch of lily pads abuts a flat of underwater weeds, thus forming one of the most productive edges in many warm-water lakes.

will harbor its share of fish, the edge of that bed where it abuts an area of pondweed will be far more attractive to fish. The deep-water edges of lily-pad patches prove time and again to hold more fish than their interiors—except around the edges of a hole. Holes in lily-pad patches may be the result of a large rock that prevents plant growth, a sudden deepening of the water, an isolated change in bottom composition, or other causes. In any case, an edge is created, and the savvy angler will not pass it by without working his lure through the spot.

Edges are also structure, which doubles their significance to fish. Although edges usually augment the population of an area by broadening the food chain, they also provide a real physical feature to which fish

Here can be seen the edge formed by lily pads and a bed of coontail, the tips of which are just visible above the surface.

The shoreline is the most obvious edge in a lake, along with the surface and the bottom. Here, the undercut bank provides important cover.

The edge formed by sunlight and shade can be of major significance to the angler on some days. Don't ignore it.

can relate. So, not only are there more fish to be found along edges because there is more food potential, but the increase of structure will support a greater number of larger fish that would otherwise be driven away by a few dominant individuals. In other words, edges accommodate more fish.

The edge formed by the borders of different types of weed beds is an obvious one. But there are numerous edges throughout a warm-water lake that are fully as significant, at various times, to the fish, yet far less obvious to the angler.

The most important edges in a lake are those formed where the water itself runs into other environments. The surface, the bottom, and the shorelines are the strongest and most significant edges for the fish, for it is there that their world ends. Fish strongly relate to those three edges in changing ways at different times of the day and year.

Edges are formed where any environment sharply meets another. Edges of sunlight and shade are often important to fish, and therefore to fishermen. Likewise, any sudden line from clear water to murky, warm to cold, moving to still (as where a stream enters a lake), wind-ruffled to glassy-smooth. Other important edges are formed where bottom features abruptly change from sandy to silty, level to uneven, bare to weedy, light to dark, bouldered to graveled.

The more edges the better. A patch of lily pads that abuts a bed of pondweed at the edge of a dropoff is great. But if it also includes a group of boulders and a fallen tree, you have the makings of a fishing spot that should cause the hair on the back of your neck to stand up and dance.

This patch of open water that forms the edge along the shoreline, emergent weeds, surface weeds, and a stump is a likely spot for excellent fishing.

You now have a useful understanding of the setting in which fish live, an understanding essential to your ability to find fish whenever you seek to catch them. By analyzing any warm-water lake in terms of its available cover and structure and by paying particular attention to its various edges, you will be able to locate fish once you know how a few other factors in their world are causing them to relate to the cover, structure, and edges.

Cover and structure are relatively permanent in a particular lake. Once you learn where they are in the lakes you fish, you can go right to the specific physical feature of your choice at any moment. They become the constants. The variables will always be those factors like time of day, time of year, weather conditions, and so on, that are different each time you fish the lake.

Here is an excellent edge between emergent weeds and surface weeds.

This productive edge borders two different types of surface weeds and a brushy bank.

Even when you fish an unfamiliar lake, the specific types of cover and structure that you know from familiar lakes will have the same significance to the fish in this new lake. And the fish will relate to them according to the same variables of time, season, weather. In other words, if you evaluate all the variables and determine that the fish should be in the weeds at the edges of dropoffs, then finding the weedy edges of the dropoffs in the unfamiliar lake will be your main concern. You may not know where they are, but you know that they are what you want to find. That hunch puts you way out ahead of ninety percent of the other anglers on the water.

Now you need to learn about the variables.

3

Light

There is no variable in the fishing equation more mercurial than light. The quality of the light coming from the sky can change, almost nonstop, from minute to minute during a partially cloudy day. But even when atmospheric conditions are stable, the routine voyage of the sun across the sky will have at least an hourly effect on the relative locations of shaded and unshaded areas in a lake. Yet those noteworthy aspects of light are inconsequential when compared to some of its less perceptible effects.

The sun is the source of all light relevant to fishing. Light, therefore, supplies three elements important to fish: heat, ultraviolet rays, and visible light. And there is more to those than meets the eye.

57

Heat

Direct sunlight for more hours per day in the summer causes lake waters to warm. In the winter, waters cool as a result of oblique sunlight for fewer hours per day. That is pretty basic; sunlight produces heat.

Each species of fish has a range of water temperatures in which it thrives. It also has a somewhat broader range of temperatures in which it can exist at all. That is to say that a fish's metabolism may work most efficiently in water between, say, sixty-three and seventy-two degrees Fahrenheit. But that fish can survive in water as cold as forty degrees and as hot as ninety degrees. Beyond those extremes, it will die. Narrower than its ideal temperature, however, is its spawning temperature. This same theoretical fish may spawn only at temperatures between sixty-five and sixty-eight degrees Fahrenheit.

In spring and fall, the seasons of most rapid changes in water temperatures, those portions of a lake that warm the fastest in spring and cool the slowest in fall are important. In summer, when water temperatures are more stable, other considerations caused by light become more significant.

During the seasonal changes in which the water is changing temperature, a lake never warms or cools uniformly throughout. Depth, bottom composition and color, the presence or absence of boulders and weeds, water clarity, and shoreline considerations create differences in the temperature of the water in any particular spot within a lake.

In terms of light as a source of heat, then, these factors are to be kept in mind:

- Except where they become lethal, summer water temperatures in warm-water lakes are of less concern to both fish and fisherman than water temperatures in spring and fall.
- In spring and fall, fish tend to seek the warmer waters within their comfort range. Food and cover, however, still influence where those warmer waters are sought.
- Because the sun is so far south during fall, winter, and spring, and because the coldest winds come from the northwestern quadrant, the warmest water during those seasons will usually be found in the northwest corner of the lake. Trees along that shoreline shield the water from cod winds, and the angle of the sun affords the most heat to that sector, just as it does to south-facing hillsides.
- Areas with dark bottoms warm better than others. Notice I did not say they warm faster. In fact, light-colored rocky areas warm faster, heating the water both as the light enters and again as it exits after being reflected back out. But dark, mucky bottoms *absorb* light and heat from the sun, releasing the heat slowly and keeping the water warmer even throughout the cool nights of spring and fall.
- In summer, the water under dense surface weeds is usually cooler than nearby open water but warmer than water shaded by overhanging trees or docks. That is because the surface weeds shade the water below them, thus keeping them cooler than water heated directly by sunlight, but they do conduct heat downward eventually, unlike shade-providing objects that do not actually touch the water.

Ultraviolet Rays and Visible Light

Suntans and sunburns are the products of ultraviolet rays. An excess of those rays is capable of causing as much discomfort to fish as to humans. Ultraviolet rays are just beyond the blue and violet end of the visible-light spectrum.

Variations in the amount of ultraviolet light penetrating the surface of a lake are dependent mainly on time of day (position of the sun), weather, and water clarity.

During the hours of dawn and dusk, when the sun is at its functional lowest, both visible light and ultraviolet rays are at their lowest as well. The misconstruction of that concurrence has resulted in one of the most popular falsehoods of fishing. The fallacy continues to be spread that fish, notably bass, are most easily caught at dawn and dusk. Many still believe that fish shun daylight because it hurts their eyes, which they cannot close for lack of eyelids. That is nonsense. The truth is that eyelids are for the sole purpose of keeping the eyes moist, a service underwater creatures are furnished automatically by their environment. Tadpoles, which live under water, do not have eyelids, yet the frogs they become, which live in the air, do. If eyelids served any other purpose than to moisten the eyes, you can bet that after umpteen million years of evolution, tadpoles and fish would have them.

It is not the sunlight in general that hurts the fishes' eyes, but the ultraviolet rays in particular that make the fish generally uncomfortable, much as excessive ultraviolet rays eventually make people uncomfortable.

At any rate, the relative paucity of ultraviolet rays during dawn and dusk affords fish the opportunity to leave those places of protection in which they hunker when the rays are stronger during the day. That tends to give anglers the impression that times of low light are better for fishing when, in fact, more fish are caught around midday. Doug Hannon—naturalist, bass expert, and meticulous keeper of records—has found that the vast majority of his five-hundred-plus trophy bass were caught between 10 A.M. and 3 P.M., and that is not surprising.

Most fish do not see as well in low light as in full daylight. That is evident in the physical makeup of their eyes which, like ours, have retinas composed of rods and cones. The cones differentiate colors, and the rods allow the eyes to function in dim light. Animals like owls, which hunt in low light, have a preponderance of rods, but few cones. Creatures that operate best in daylight, like us, have lots of cones at the expense of rods. Most of the fish you will encounter follow that plan, as is proved by the difference a subtle change in lure color can make. Fish are most likely to take prey when they can see best, and that is when the light is good. (By the way, dawn and dusk fishing have their undisputed pleasures; air temperatures are comfortable, the wind is calm, the water is glassy, wildlife abounds, waterskiers and boaters have yet to upset the stillness, and the fish are less spooky and more noticeable. But avoid confusing all that with better fishing.)

Perhaps of most importance to the amount of ultraviolet rays reaching fish is the weather—specifically, the amount of moisture in the air. The average relative humidity of a June day in Boston is seventy-two per-

cent at eight o'clock in the morning and fifty-nine percent at noon. In Columbus, Ohio, it is seventy-seven
percent at seven-thirty in the morning and fifty-eight
percent at noon. That same day in Miami would average seventy-five percent and sixty-nine percent. As a
matter of fact, in very few places in the non-arid areas
of this country does the average relative humidity for
any month throughout the entire year fall below fifty
percent. In the summer months, it is usually much
higher. That means that, on the average, the air is
holding from half to three-quarters of the moisture it
can possibly hold at that particular temperature—the
higher the temperature, the more moisture can be held
in suspension. That much moisture in the air does an
excellent job of diffusing ultraviolet rays and keeping
their level from getting uncomfortable; fish do not have
to bury themselves in dense cover to avoid the rays during days of normal humidity.

During those periods immediately following a cold
front, however, when the sky is deep blue and cloudless
and, even in summer, the air feels fresh and clean, the
relative humidity may go down to thirty percent or
much less. There are no clouds and little moisture in
the air to scatter the ultraviolet light. Fish disappear
as though by magic, so eagerly do they seek cover from
the discomfort. Where weeds are available, the fish go
right down to the bottom of the growth and hide among
the densest parts. If the cover is not sufficient, fish will
go to deeper water, beyond the penetration of the harsh
rays. It is not uncommon, during cold-front conditions,
to find the fish fifteen to twenty feet deeper than usual
in very clear water. If the water is murky or stained,
the ultraviolet rays will not penetrate as well, and the

fish need not go down so far. When the humidity once again begins to rise and the merciless blueness of the sky is softened by a hint of haze, the fish will resume normal activity.

Make no mistake, the fish do not refuse to eat during those low-humidity conditions. But they do refuse to leave their refuges. Lures dropped on their noses will be greedily accepted. Most anglers, however, simply find the fishing so difficult that they give up, believing that the fish have turned off completely.

Here are a few points to remember about the effects of ultraviolet rays on fish:

- Overcast days and days of high humidity reduce the ultraviolet discomfort. Fish are less tightly bound to cover.
- Midday on a sunny day with lots of humidity is the best time to go after big fish. Their vision is best because of the excellent light, but they are not tight to cover, the humidity having reduced the discomfort of the ultraviolet rays.
- On normal sunny days, fish will seek the shady side of cover and structure. The shade hides them from both enemy and prey and shelters them from ultraviolet rays.
- In cold-front conditions, fish will be *under* cover, not merely on the shady side of it. Excessive ultraviolet will be reflected from the entire blue sky, not just the area where the sun is.
- When the ultraviolet light's penetration is low, fish can be coaxed to the surface for a lure. When it is high, you have to go down and find them.
- Fishing at night can be productive for some species.

The trick is to make use of the fact that the sky, even at its darkest, is never as dark as the bottom of the lake. A dark surface lure, therefore, will be silhouetted against the sky, and night-feeding fish will be attracted to it by its noise. Bass, bluegills, sunfish, crappies, and white perch will eat at night. Pickerel and yellow perch seem not to. The advantages of fishing at night are that the lack of any ultraviolet discomfort, the relative safety from enemies, and the abatement of human recreational noises allow fish to roam the shallows with greater freedom and less caution. You will also probably have the lake to yourself.

Those are the most important aspects of light's effect on your fish-finding decisions. By making an assessment of the light's significance at any particular time—in terms of how and where it is heating the water and how the fish are most likely reacting to those water temperatures, the ultraviolet rays, and the visible light—and adding that to your understanding of structure, cover, and edges, you begin to progress toward an informed opinion of where the fish can be found. And that will lead to a plan for the day.

First, though, you have to know about another crucial variable—the seasonal influence.

4

A Fish's Yearly Calendar

THE SEASONAL VARIABLE

If Lake Tepidaqua were located in some magical place where the temperature of the air remained constant all year, the number of hours of daylight never varied, and the fish had no concerns besides personal survival, you would now have sufficient knowledge to go out onto its bounteous waters and find fish at any time of the day during any day of the year.

All you would have to do is locate the most productive edges of the best areas of cover—they would almost never vary; the fish would be constantly in association with those—and determine the fish's likely attitude within those areas according to the effects of ultraviolet and visible light. Simple. Even without considering the light at all, you would never be off by more than a few feet.

Here in reality, however, the air temperature and hours of daylight change with the seasons, causing an often radical metamorphosis to the environment in which fish live. And the fish themselves spend part of their year preoccupied with a drive to procreate. Those seasonal considerations play havoc with the potential simplicity of understanding fish behavior.

Anyone who has ever traveled between New England and south Florida during March can appreciate the inadequacy of calendar dates for describing events in nature. The first day of spring in Massachusetts is often indistinguishable from the dead of winter, while that same day in Fort Lauderdale may look like the peak of New England summer. By mid-March in south Florida, male largemouth bass have cleared their platter-sized nests in the warm shallows and are coaxing the huge and gravid females into position for spawning. In New England, that behavior may not occur for another three months, well after the ice melts and the temperature of the water rises another thirty degrees.

Yet once the New England fish *are* moved to perform any particular seasonal behavior, they will react identically to the way their Floridian counterparts behaved several months earlier. That allows us to conveniently express a fish's year-round behavior in terms of significant events and seasonal developments common to the warm-water lakes of the entire country *even if those events and developments occur at widely differing times in different lakes.* In other words, no matter where your personal Lake Tepidaqua resides, the fish in its waters will be living their lives according to a local yearly calendar that contains six main parts: cold water; pre-spawn; the spawning period; post-spawn; summer; and fall, returning again to cold water.

Cold Water

As I've pointed out, everything is relative. But in most warm-water lakes throughout the country, there comes a time during the winter when the water temperature falls below a crucial level. At that level, many of the fish species in the lake experience a metabolic slowdown; they are less active and require less food. Largemouth bass, for example, experience a significant slowdown in their metabolic rate below about fifty-five degrees Fahrenheit. Yellow perch, however, seem to barely slow at all and remain eager to hit a lure lowered through the ice.

In any case, the cold water period is characterized by the year's lowest level of activity in the lake for predators, prey, and plants as well. In the South that may be a couple of weeks in January when the water is still comfortable for humans to swim in. In the North, it may be five months, during which time the surface of the lake will support truck traffic.

Pre-spawn

Different species of fish spawn at different times within the same lake. Spawning is triggered by water temperature. Pickerel and yellow perch, for example, are moved to lay their eggs when the temperature of the water is still only in the high forties. Bass and bluegills, on the other hand, will not even begin to start clearing nests until the water temperature reaches about sixty. Given that bit of specific natural history (of which there will be more in the next chapter), it is easy to see that the pre-spawn period of pickerel (the transitional time between cold water and spawning) will be a lot shorter than that of bass.

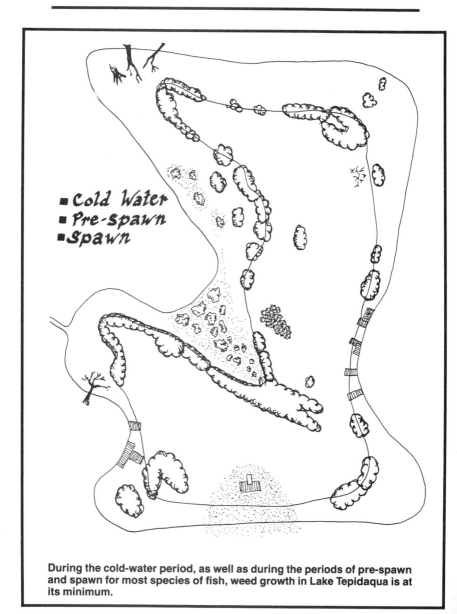

Cold Water
Pre-spawn
Spawn

During the cold-water period, as well as during the periods of pre-spawn and spawn for most species of fish, weed growth in Lake Tepidaqua is at its minimum.

Nonetheless, the pre-spawn period for most species is characterized by a rise in water temperature and a corresponding increase in metabolism. Insects and hibernating food species start to become active, but are few and far between. Cover is thin and sparse. Fish are hungry, not yet preoccupied with sex, and will readily hit lures and baits. Fish tend to seek protected, sun-warmed shallows by day and retreat to deep water at night and during cold, cloudy, or rainy days.

The Spawning Period

This is a tightly temperature-controlled time slot for any species. It is usually brief, mainly because the rapidly warming water at this time of year remains within a species' spawning range for only a few days. During that time, spawning will take place where conditions in the lake are favorable. That means that if a species requires a sandy bottom and a water temperature of around sixty-two degrees for spawning, sandy areas in the northwest corner of the lake will see spawning activity from that species earlier than sandy areas in the southern portion of the lake. All individuals of a species throughout a lake, therefore, will not be spawning at once, and what is actually a brief period for any one individual fish, may appear to be a longer period for a species throughout a lake.

Some species clear nests on the bottom of a lake, while others merely broadcast their eggs over bottom vegetation. Some species are done with spawning immediately upon ridding themselves of eggs and milt, some protect the eggs only until they hatch, and others

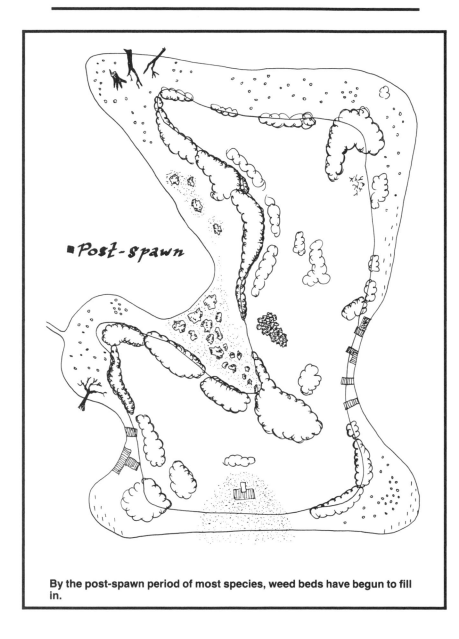

By the post-spawn period of most species, weed beds have begun to fill in.

render some measure of parental care to the hatchlings.

The spawning period of any species is a time of intense activity but generally poor fishing; eating becomes pitifully secondary to other considerations.

Post-spawn

Once the rigors of spawning are done, fish tend to need a short period of rest and recuperation. Whether a species simply dumps its eggs and calls it quits, or spends a lot of time claiming territory, clearing a nest, and guarding its young, the effort expended merely in laying and fertilizing eggs is enough to necessitate at least a short period of recovery. In many species, females require a bit more time than males to get back to the business of eating and chasing prey. In some species, the males stay on the nests to protect the eggs until the hatchlings can find their own cover.

The post-spawn period of a species is characterized by low levels of activity and nonspecific behavior. The single-minded activity of spawning, followed by recuperation, gives way to a general but desultory exodus from the shallow spawning areas into what little cover is beginning to regenerate in the lake. Weed beds are still patchy, baitfish are scattered, newborn fry are tiny and difficult to find, and the fish of a particular species are all over the lake, some still spawning, others finished, and a few having not yet gotten around to it. Fishing is poor, but steadily improving.

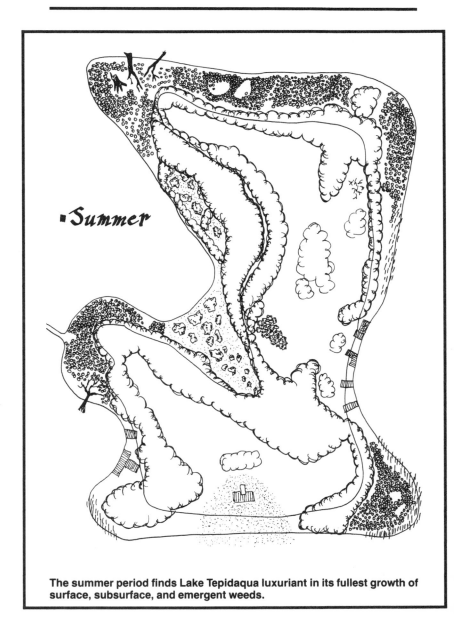

Summer

The summer period finds Lake Tepidaqua luxuriant in its fullest growth of surface, subsurface, and emergent weeds.

Summer

This is the time when most people fish. The lake has finally acquired its full growth of weeds—subsurface beds are dense and lush, lily-pad patches have filled in and offer broad expanses of unbroken cover, and emergent vegetation is at its peak. For most warmwater species, this is a time of extreme stability. There will, of course, be movement of most species from deeper cover to shallows during the safety of darkness, and whatever movement is necessary for comfort and protection, but fish will generally remain in specific areas throughout this period.

At the start of this period, cover is abundant but food is scarce; newborn fry are well hidden, and populations of insects, frogs, and other prey have not yet exploded. Fishing is at its best. As the summer period advances and matures, food becomes plentiful and fishing remains excellent, but because fish have so much natural food and cover is so lush, it is more difficult to tempt them with lures and even live bait. While careful, knowledgeable, and patient anglers continue to find plentiful success, less astute fishermen succumb to misconceptions about its being too hot to fish or, worse yet, about the lake being fished out.

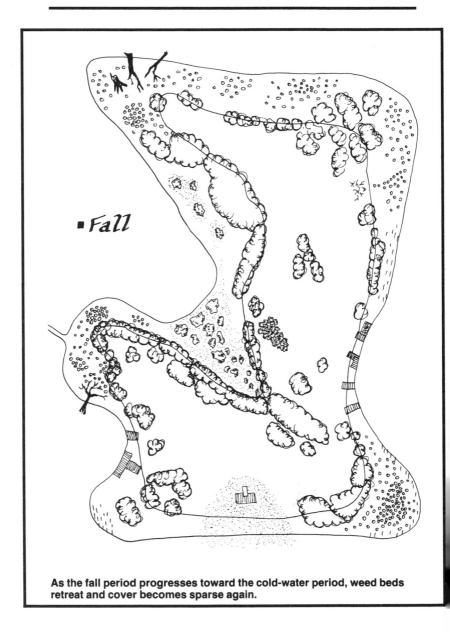

As the fall period progresses toward the cold-water period, weed beds retreat and cover becomes sparse again.

Fall

Roughly corresponding to the actual calendar season, the fall period in the life of a lake will see the deterioration of plant growth due, mainly, to fewer hours of daylight. In many areas, too, nights will become cool enough to begin lowering the temperature of the water. Eventually, plant growth declines perceptively and begins to provide inadequate cover—lily-pad patches become ragged and full of holes and open spaces; subsurface weed beds thin like a middle-aged pate.

With the cover offering less protection and food extremely abundant—the young of the year, in most cases, have by now reached a size that makes a very decent meal—fish feed voraciously and are not at all fastidious. Lures are taken as readily as natural foods.

As the weed cover continues to disappear from the shallows and flats, offering poor protection from the bright, sparkling days that can occur with great frequency in fall and winter, fish will rely on deeper water for relief from ultraviolet rays. Still, though, they will roam the shallower waters for food. Finding the fish becomes more difficult. Ultimately, they visit the shallows less frequently and take up cold water positions off the dropoffs or in remaining green weed beds.

Eventually, the surface water cools to the point where it sinks and warmer water from below rises to the surface. This is called the Fall Turnover. In lakes that stratify into the three temperature zones, the turnover breaks down those stratifications and mixes the water into homogeneity. But even lakes that do not stratify undergo some degree of turnover. In most cases, the water becomes moderately to extremely turbid from the disturbed bottom debris, and fishing becomes terrible. Luckily, things settle down within a few days.

Turnover is usually followed by a continued cooling of the water to the point where the lake enters its cold-water period.

It is important to understand that this yearly calendar represents the schedule of an ecological system; some of the phases are defined by the activities of the particular species of fish in question (in which case it may not at all coincide with the period in which other species are involved at the time), and other phases are defined by the condition of the environment—the lake itself—and will therefore affect all resident species similarly.

The following chart may help to sort some of that out and provide a quick reference to some of the aspects of the calendar periods.

One other important consideration to keep in mind when analyzing calendar periods is that any particular period may vary greatly in character from year to year, even within the same lake. The pre-spawn period, for example, which is influenced by water temperature and day length, may be very different in a year of extended cold rains from a year with a mild winter and early warm weather. In one case weed growth, which is more influenced by light than temperature, may be well on its way before the shallows come anywhere near reaching a temperature comfortable for pre-spawn movements of some fish. On the other hand, a hot early spring may find fish well up in the shallows before the weeds have gained much ground. In the two cases, both pre-spawn, your fishing strategy will have to be very different. In the first case, the banks provide the only cover; in the latter, the weeds are more important.

The same kind of thing can happen in fall. Cold rains and an early winter can drive fish well toward their cold-water period while cover in the shallows is still quite lush. Conversely, a late fall with a lingering Indian summer can find weeds all but gone from the flats while fish are bunched up around the remaining clumps.

That all means that your powers of observation and ability to use that information intelligently are always your most important fishing tools. Don't allow yourself to be trapped in the kind of dead-end thinking that most inferior anglers use: If it worked last year, it'll work again this year.

CALENDAR PERIODS	CONDITION OF LAKE
COLD WATER	Lowest level of activity and coldest water temperatures of year.
PRE-SPAWN	Warming from cold water period. Little weed cover, scarce food.
SPAWN	Warming but variable. This period is entirely dependent on species.
POST-SPAWN	Variable depending on when species spawns.
SUMMER	Maximum weed growth, densest cover, plentiful aquatic life. Peak of activity.
FALL	Less daylight and cooler temperatures slow plant and animal activity. Food is abundant but cover is thinning. Cooling water turns over, then cools further into cold water period.

BEHAVIOR OF FISH	QUALITY OF FISHING
Metabolisms slow to minimum of year. Some species still active. Some move to deep water.	Variable. Food needs decline with metabolic rate. Slow presentation essential.
Fish seeking food and warmest water. Constant back-and-forth movement between shallows and deeper water.	Excellent. But finding the fish may be difficult. Locations often change daily, sometimes hourly.
Entirely preoccupied with mating. Some on nests, others simply broadcasting eggs.	Poor. Some species should be left alone.
Fish, especially females, recuperating from stress of mating. Some males remain on nests.	Period begins with poor fishing and ends with superb fishing as fish regain strength, aggressiveness, and a hunger not met by prey availability.
Establishment of stable routines and areas of concentration in specific cover and structure.	Excellent. But abundance of natural food and growth of dense cover requires more skill of anglers.
Fish feed on abundant prey in sparse cover and store energy for cold-water period. Movement back and forth between shallows and dropoffs. Metabolisms begin to slow as temperature drops.	Superb until turnover, then poor until lake settles.

5

Some Fish

UP CLOSE AND PICKEREL

Now, in addition to your understanding of cover, structure, edges, the effects of light, and the fact that fish undergo a succession of seasonal changes of behavior, you must learn some basic and painless facts about a few of the specific types of fish you are most likely to encounter in Lake Tepidaqua.

This will not be an exhaustive course in icthyological ethology. There are plenty of excellent sources of highly specific information on the natural history of specific fish and their behaviors. What you should have, however, is a rudimentary knowledge of the differences (and similarities) among a few warm-water species so that you can more successfully catch the ones you set out to catch. You might want to know, for example, that looking for spawning yellow perch in seventy-degree water is a waste of time, or that pre-spawn bluegills can be found in shallow water, but not necessarily near areas in which they will nest.

The point is that the few types of fish you will meet all share a general environment and way of life, but they are all different—sometimes only subtly—when it comes down to specifics. It therefore helps to have an idea of what the various species are doing during the calendar periods. Keep in mind, now, that the calendar periods are defined by two perspectives: some periods reflect events in the general environment—cold-water is the *lake's* time of minimum plant and animal activity, while summer is its maximum—and other periods like pre-spawn, spawn, and post-spawn are determined by precise events in the lives of specific kinds of *fish*. I'll keep you oriented to those perspectives during the following discussion. All temperatures are in degrees Fahrenheit and indicate the temperature of the water's surface, not the air.

Basses and Sunfishes

The majority of the species you will encounter in warm-water lakes are members of the sunfish family. Those include—depending on the exact characteristics of the lake and its geographical location—the large-mouth and smallmouth basses, bluegills, pumpkin-seeds, a variety of panfish actually called sunfishes, black and white crappies, rock bass, and warmouths.

As a result of their kinship, many of those species share certain habits; all tend to relate closely to a home territory or specific structure as opposed to roaming widely, as do some of the other species you will meet. Yet, even though closely related, each species has its own habits and idiosyncracies that become relevant to an angler's success in finding them at any particular time.

Rather than detail all thirty species of basses and sunfishes that occur throughout North America, I will briefly introduce you to the six species that the greatest number of anglers are likely to meet: the largemouth bass, smallmouth bass, bluegill, pumpkinseed, black crappie, and white crappie.

Largemouth Bass

General Habits and Habitat: Young fish school, and larger fish are inclined to form loose schools as well, more so in clear water where they can keep in visual contact. Largest individuals tend to be solitary, especially in murky water. All largemouths relate strongly to structure, which may include cover or bottom topography. Large structures, like dropoffs and points, can concentrate a lot of bass that would otherwise be inclined to disperse. Largemouths eat all smaller fish, frogs, crayfish, insects, mice, snakes, ducklings—in short, just about anything they can inhale.

COLD WATER

(Lowest temperatures of the year)

This is a time of minimum activity for both the lake and the bass. Generally speaking, largemouths will be suspended in the deepest parts of the lake, relating to deep structure such as the deep ends of points and whatever clumps of green weeds they can find. They will eat during this period, but their metabolism and level of activity is reduced, especially below fifty-five degrees.

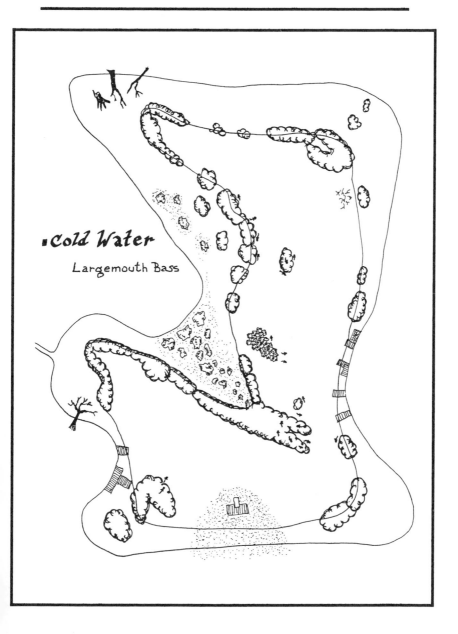

Cold Water

Largemouth Bass

PRE-SPAWN

(Approximately 50° to approximately 60°)

Warming water will start the bass toward shallow, protected, spawning areas, but highly variable spring weather will have them yo-yoing back and forth between deep and shallow waters. Bass will tend to move along the shortest routes between prime spawning areas and deep water sanctuaries.

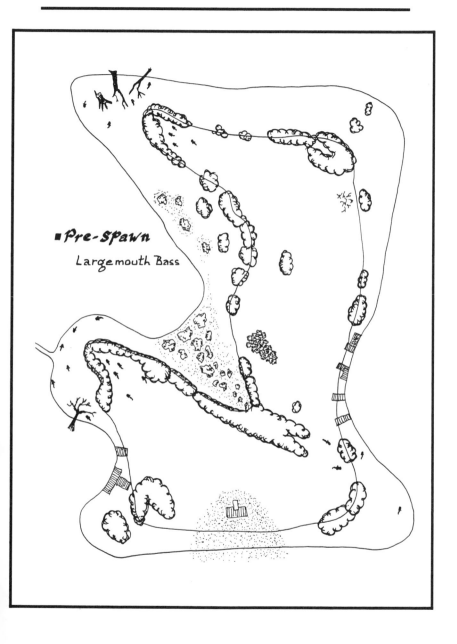

Pre-Spawn

Largemouth Bass

THE SPAWNING PERIOD

(62° to 65° is the ideal)

Males fan out a platter-shaped nest, preferably in gravel. The nest is typically about a foot and a half in diameter and is located in about two feet of water not far from shore. Where suitable spawning habitat is plentiful, largemouth nests tend to be well separated from one another by several feet, but can become quite close together where territory is limited. Females join the males on the nests and spawning takes place. The males stay and guard the eggs after the females have left.

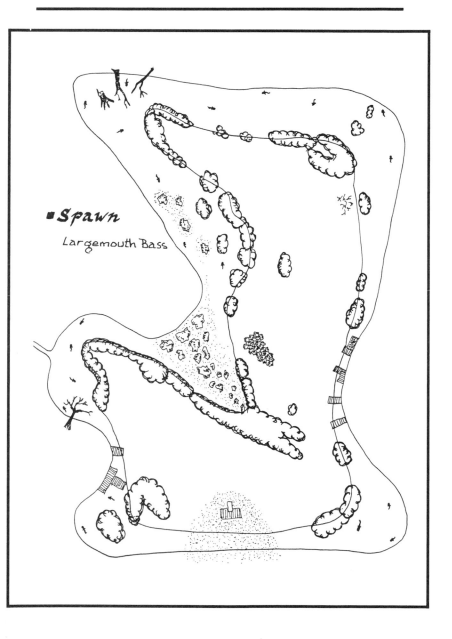

Spawn

Largemouth Bass

POST-SPAWN

(From the conclusion of spawning to full weed growth)

The eggs hatch in about a week, and the male bass stay on the nests and guard the fry. The females, in need of rest from the spawning ordeal, retire to the deeper-water sanctuaries once again. At this time, vegetation is just beginning to develop and food is scattered. Bass eat little at first, concentrating on recuperation, but they soon take up the pursuit of food with single-minded diligence. As the season progresses toward full summer, the lake's vegetation begins to mature and create areas in which food will concentrate. In the meantime, the bass tend to be scattered along with the food supply and are a bit difficult to locate with any dependability.

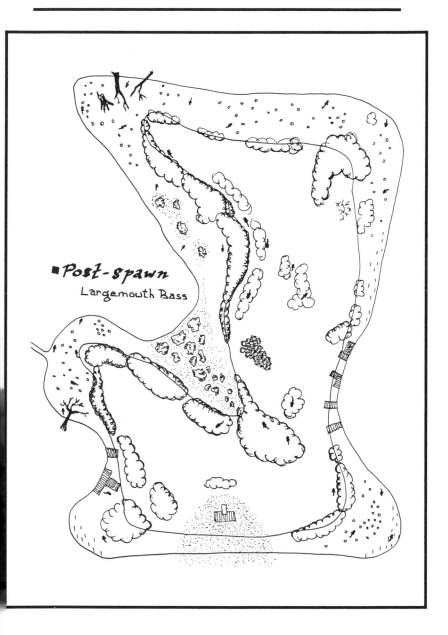

SUMMER

(The lake's period of peak activity and maximum temperatures)

Natural food is abundant and cover is lush. Bass tend to settle down into stable locations of cover in areas of concentrated food. For many bass, that will be on the shallow flats in five to ten feet of water. Others will remain in the shallows under cover of dense mats of surface weeds.

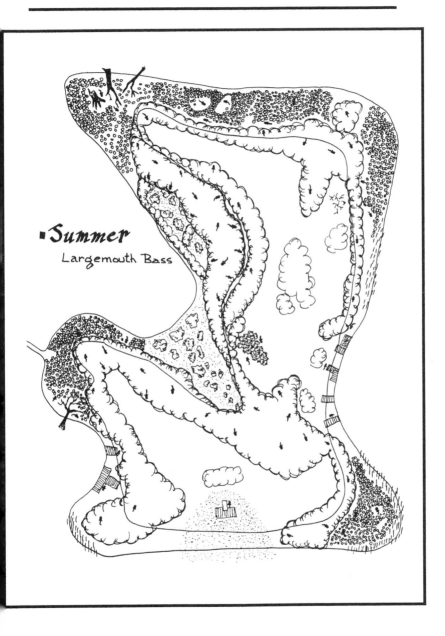

Summer

Largemouth Bass

FALL

(From the first cooling trend down to about 50°)

As the water begins to cool and day length decreases, cover begins to thin. Once again, as in spring, vagaries of the weather drive the bass back and forth between the dropoffs and the shallows. Now though, food is abundant, and in preparation for the winter slowdown, bass go on a feeding binge. Points, which provide a natural connection between shallow water and deep, will see congregations of bass. Gradually, the surface water cools enough to sink, and the turnover occurs, throwing the lake into turmoil and turning off the bass. After the turnover, the lake and the bass slow down in a gradual but steady shift toward the cold-water period; the bass move toward deeper water, their metabolism slows, they eat less often, and shift to smaller forage.

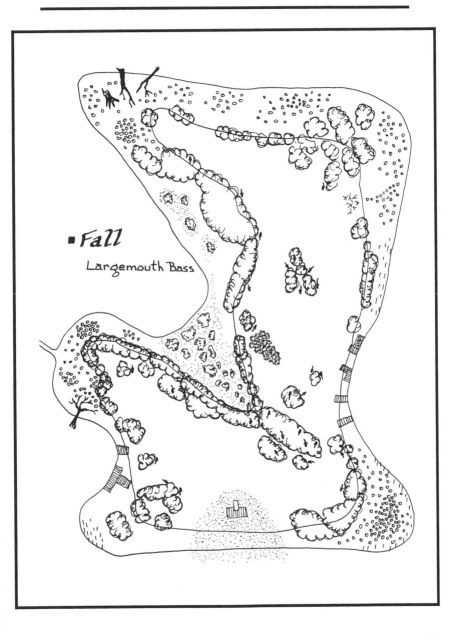

■ *Fall*

Largemouth Bass

Smallmouth Bass

General Habits and Habitat: Warm-water lakes often hold no smallmouths at all, which are far more abundant in rivers and ecologically younger lakes where they have no competition from largemouths. In warm-water lakes where smallies do occur, however, they will surely be sharing the environment with largemouth bass. But because the largemouths are always the dominant species of the two, smallmouth bass in warm-water lakes will typically be forced to occupy the rocky areas, which largemouths find less habitable. Under those conditions, the smallies' diet consists largely of crayfish, hellgrammites, and baitfish.

COLD WATER

(Lowest temperatures of the year)

During this time of the coldest water temperatures of the year, smallmouth bass school in deep water in rocky, hard-bottom areas. Typically, they may suspend along a steep dropoff or over a rocky hump at depths of thirty feet or more. They feed only sporadically.

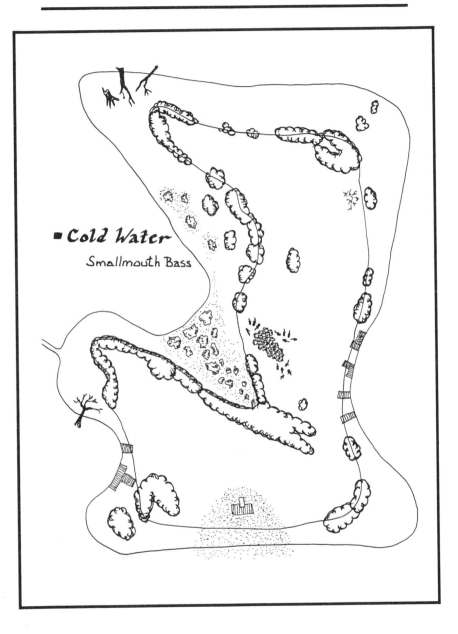

PRE-SPAWN

(Approximately 35° to approximately 55°)

While still remaining deep, the bass will begin a general movement toward the spawning areas. Not until the water temperature reaches the midforties, however, will the smallies actually start up into shallow water. They begin to seek the gravel- or rubble-bottomed sheltered coves in which they will spawn, but their initial activities involve the search for food. At this time, the bass are extremely aggressive. As the temperatures creep up into the fifties, the aggressive feeding behavior lessens and all action turns toward spawning. The males fan out nests, typically in about three feet of water near some piece of structure (a rock or fallen log), while the females slip back into slightly deeper water again.

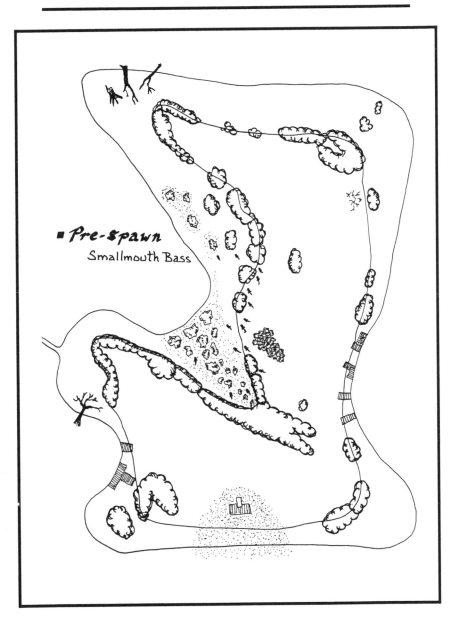

■ *Pre-spawn*
Smallmouth Bass

THE SPAWNING PERIOD

(56° to 64° is the ideal)

Once the males have prepared the nests and the conditions are right, the females move back into the shallows and are lured by the males onto the nests. After the eggs are laid, the male continues to guard them and the females move back to the deeper water again.

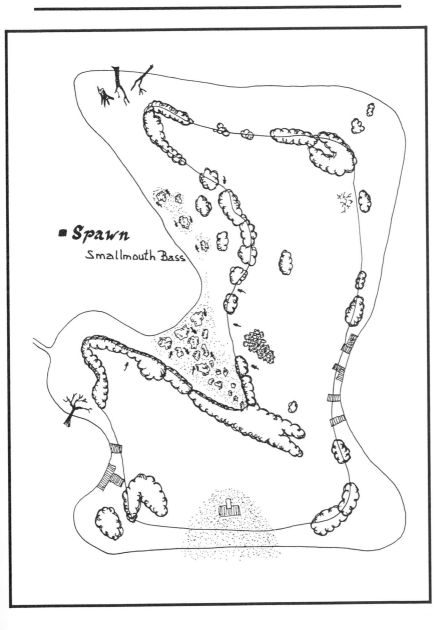

Spawn
Smallmouth Bass

POST-SPAWN

(From the conclusion of spawning to full weed growth)

As with the largemouth bass, the post-spawn period for smallies is a time first of rest and recuperation and then, gradually, of filling their bellies again. The males remain on the nests until the fry go off on their own, while the females revive in deeper water. As the lake warms and the activity of food species increases, the bass shift their orientation from sex to food. By the end of this period, they have settled into their summer locations.

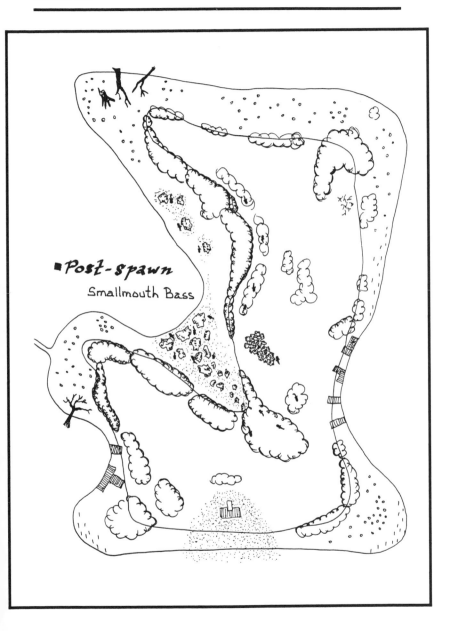

SUMMER

(The lake's period of peak activity and maximum temperatures)

Although the smallies may prefer to inhabit the weedy flats, the largemouths will undoubtedly chase them from those areas, limiting the smallies to the rocky shallows and deep-water dropoffs. Thus, in warm-water lakes like Tepidaqua, the summer period will find any resident smallmouths pretty well distributed in those rocky areas, both shallow and deep, that are of little interest to the largemouths. Rubble-bottomed flats with fallen trees and large boulders for cover will attract smallies. So will sharp breaks toward deep water where they will form schools of similarly sized individuals. Smallies that seek deep water in summer are not, as typically believed, doing so to escape the warmth of the shallows—smallies, as it turns out, can tolerate extremely warm water—but are doing so because the limited rocky flats are pretty well filled to capacity by other members of their species.

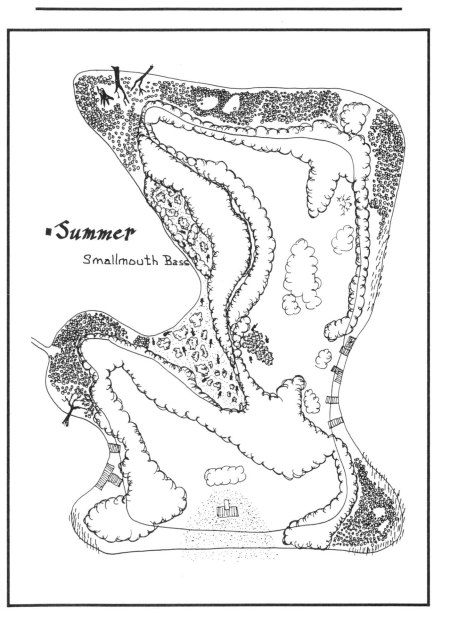

Summer

Smallmouth Bass

FALL

(From the first cooling trend down to about 50°)

The thinning of the summer's lush vegetation has less direct effect on the smallies in Lake Tepidaqua than it does on the largemouths, for the smallies have not been allowed in the areas of dense growth but have been living in the rocky areas, which are little altered by the seasonal change. But they do, of course, rely on the forage—and where the food goes, so go the bass. Thus begins a general movement to deeper water. Following the rocky points back down into the depths, the smallmouth bass gradually move toward their winter sanctuaries. Here again though, in the earlier parts of this period they will be back and forth along these routes, shallower on warm days, deeper after cold spells, as the changeable weather patterns settle into winter.

Crappies

General Habits and Habitat: There are actually two distinct species of these feisty, schooling panfish: the white and the black. The white are most prevalent in the murky manmade impoundments of the South. The black crappie predominates in the clearer natural lakes of the North. A significant exception occurs in Florida, where it is the black crappie that thrives in the clear waters. Still, there are plenty of warm-water lakes in the country's midsection where both species may be caught, although in such situations the white crappie usually does best.

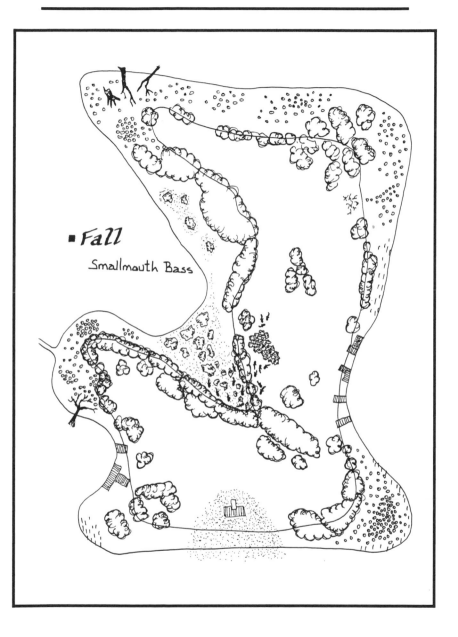

Fall

Smallmouth Bass

Crappie feed largely on minnows between one and a half and two and a half inches in length. Although schools will often travel around a lake, the fish are extremely structure-oriented and can usually be located by systematically visiting specific sites—particularly brush piles and weed beds at the edges of dropoffs— where they have been found in the past. They make particularly good eating, and their schooling habit makes them an excellent choice for supplying the makings of a fish fry; once you locate the school, you can catch large numbers. The fragile membrane around the mouth of a crappie often allows hooks to pull out easily, so care must be used in landing them.

COLD WATER

(Lowest temperatures of the year)

Crappies feed throughout the cold-water period and often provide excellent action for the northern angler fishing through the ice with live minnows or artificial jigs. Generally, the fish will be found suspended off the deeper remaining weed beds on the edges of dropoffs in about twenty feet of water, but crappies also characteristically suspend right out in the middle of the deep-water area of the lake, far from any structure.

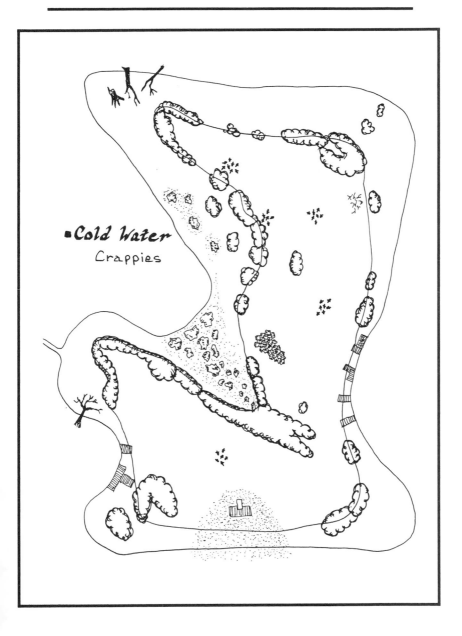

PRE-SPAWN

(Approximately 35° to approximately 50°)

At this time of unstable weather, warm calm days will find the crappies moving into sheltered coves, and cold rainy weather will push them back out to the deeper water. Generally, though, they will be following baitfish into the protected shallows that warm first, relating to existing cover such as docks and brush. This movement has nothing to do with eventual nesting areas. Pre-spawn crappies are initially concerned with food. As the water temperatures stabilize near fifty degrees, however, they will begin moving toward spawning areas.

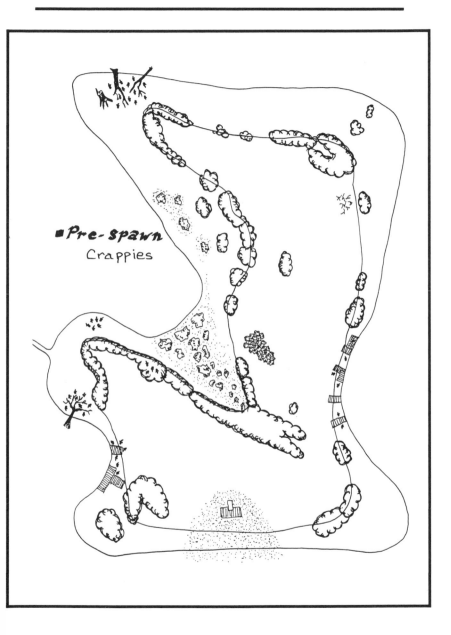

THE SPAWNING PERIOD

(64° to 68° is the ideal)

Like all sunfishes, the male is the one who selects the nest site and fans out a clearing on the bottom. Typically, that will be in a sheltered cove with a bottom of sand and plant debris, but not deep muck, and in which there is plenty of cover in the form of weeds, brush, or stumps. Crappies have been known to lay their eggs on the tops of submerged stumps and logs. The depth at which they nest is somewhat dependent on water clarity and tends to be between two and eight feet. Spawning crappies form communities in which the nests are quite close together. Although their interest is focused on pursuits other than eating, they will aggressively snap at unwelcome intruders, so lures worked through a nesting area will catch fish.

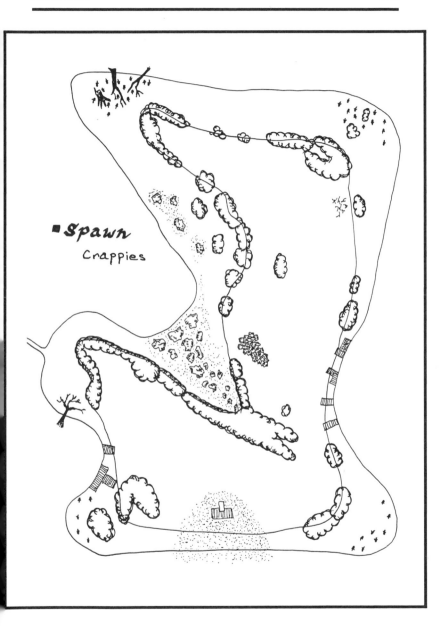

POST-SPAWN

(From the conclusion of spawning to full weed growth)

After spawning, the females scatter into deeper parts of the coves while the males tend to the young. The eggs usually hatch in a few days, but the male crappies look after the fry until the young leave the nests altogether. Then the males, too, scatter into the coves. At this time it is often difficult to locate crappies, for the schools have not yet regrouped. Eventually, though, they will form tight groups that are ready to terrorize the minnow population of the lake.

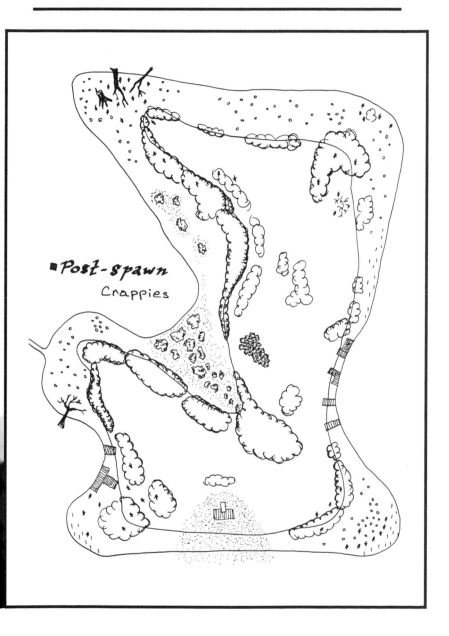

■ *Post-spawn*
Crappies

SUMMER

(The lake's period of peak activity and maximum temperatures)

Schools of crappies will now once again be found suspended near the edges of dropoffs. Weed beds and brush piles at the lips of the drops to deeper water, whether in creek channels, off points, or at the edges of flats, will hold crappies throughout the summer. That is a relatively sure thing.

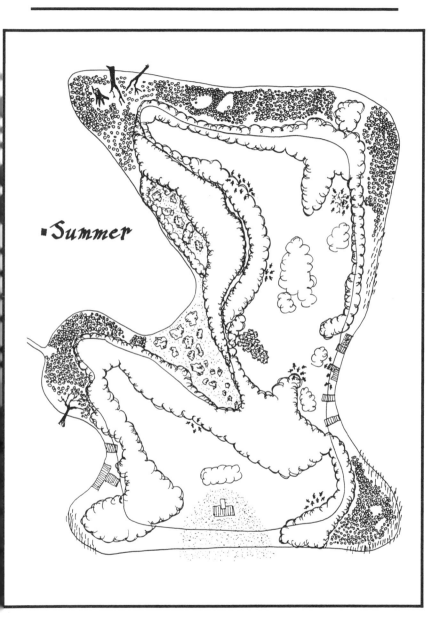

Summer

FALL

(From the first cooling trend down to the coldest water)

This transitional period between summer and cold water does not have much effect on crappies, for they are active feeders all through the winter. Generally, though, the fall period will see crappies first holding tighter to the cover near the dropoffs, often hunkering down in the weeds in response to the season's frequent cold fronts, and then moving farther off toward deep water as the water temperature decreases, suspending farther away from cover in the middle of the deep-water holes.

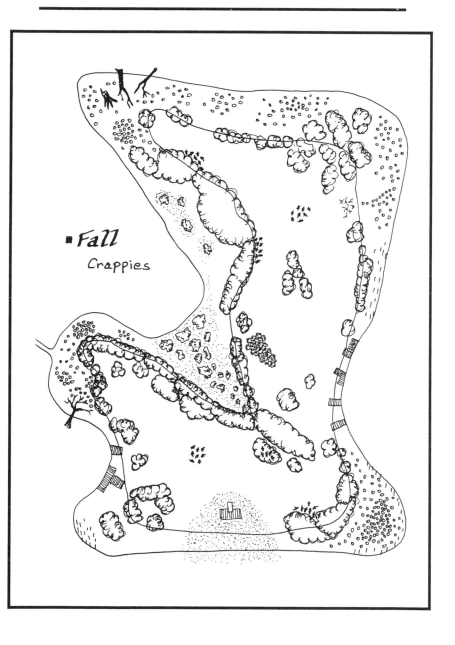

Bluegills

General Habits and Habitat: These large sunfish form schools of about ten to twenty individuals. They are undoubtedly the most popular and widespread pan-fish in the country, and make good eating. They feed largely on insects and are arguably the most important inhabitant of warm-water lakes in terms of insect control. They also feed on snails, plants, and the eggs of other fish, particularly bass. Schools do not roam around a lake, as do crappies, but stick quite tightly to a home territory.

COLD WATER
(Lowest temperatures of the year)

Like bass, the metabolism of bluegills reaches a critical point at about fifty-five degrees. Although they can be caught even through the ice, bluegills tend to eat much less frequently during this period, often subsisting on plants. Tight schools suspend at about ten to fifteen feet and move slightly shallower and deeper according to changes in the weather.

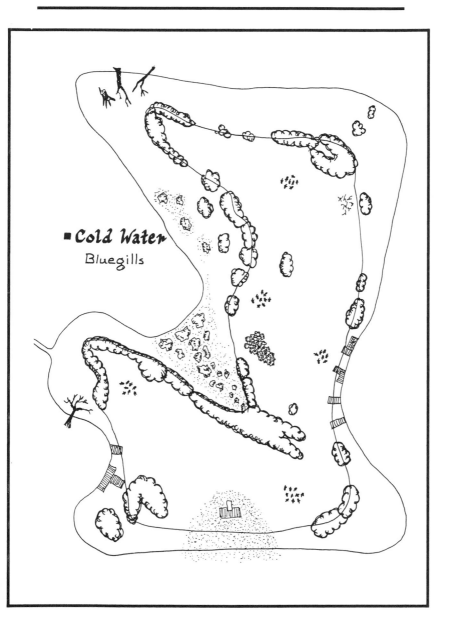

PRE-SPAWN

(Approximately 35° to approximately 60°)

After ice-out in the North, and as the water begins to warm in the South, bluegill schools break up and the individual fish begin heading for the shallows in search of warm water and food. The coves that warm the fastest will find the best concentrations of bluegills, which will follow the best cover. Cold weather will drive them back out to deep water.

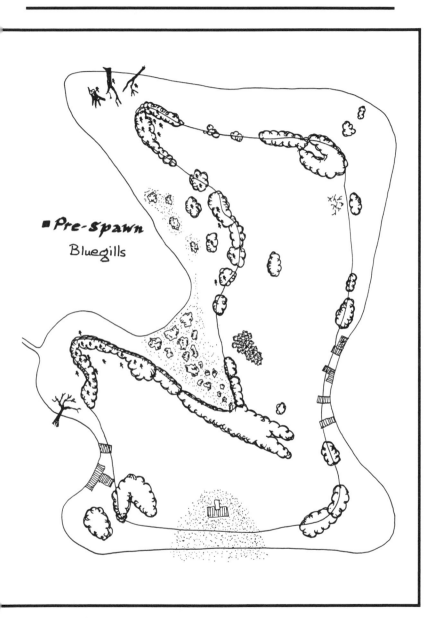

■ *Pre-spawn*
  Bluegills

THE SPAWNING PERIOD

(60° to quite variable)

Bluegills may nest in such close proximity to one another that the edges of the nests may actually touch. Shallow areas with sandy or gravelly bottoms are preferred, and you can usually see the congregations of nests quite clearly. As with all sunfish, the males clear the nest and lure the females into them for the actual mating. Because bluegill populations in a lake may be so high and competition for prime spawning areas so great, many fish put off spawning until the first wave has finished. As a result, a particularly choice area may hold spawning bluegills well into the summer period. Small fly-rod poppers dropped over a densely packed spawning area can keep you giggling with glee for hours.

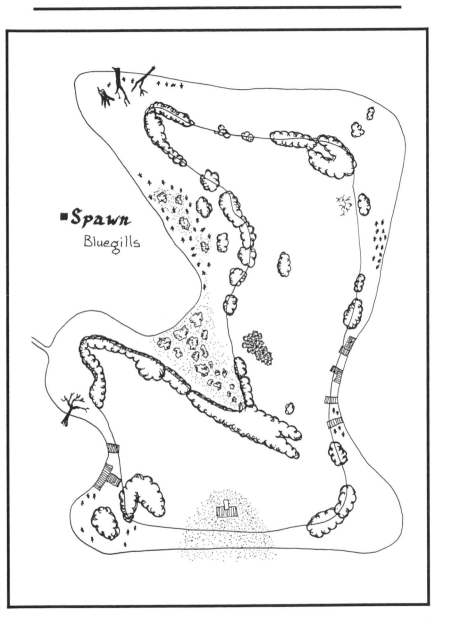

POST-SPAWN

(From the conclusion of spawning to full weed growth)

As do other sunfish, the males stay awhile to care for the young while the females scatter into deeper water to recuperate from spawning. After a few days the males join them, and the summer schools begin to form.

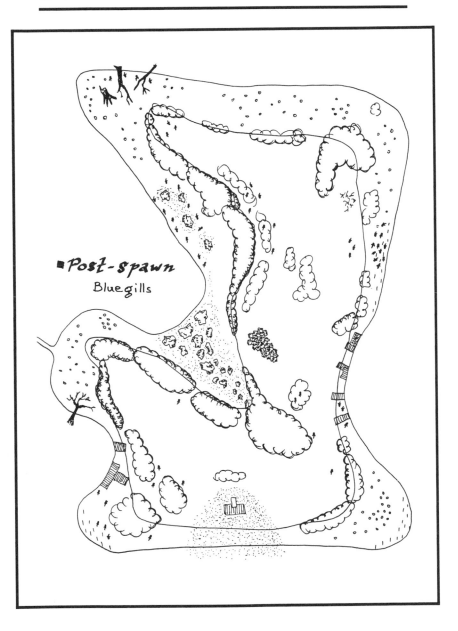

SUMMER

(The lake's period of peak activity and maximum temperatures)

During the stable summer period, bluegills remain in small schools and hold tight to specific cover and structure. During the heat of the day they stay in deeper water, strongly relating to weed beds. However, docks, rafts, and boathouses in deep water offer a potent attraction to bluegills. Areas with large boulders often draw bluegills as well. During this period there is generally a daily migration of the school to shallower water in the evening. A great deal of surface feeding on aquatic insects may occur at this time and throughout the night. Light and heat will move them deep again the next day, where they will continue feeding on subsurface insects.

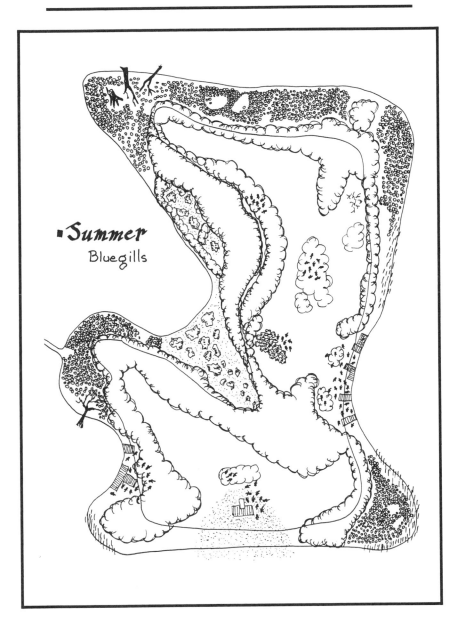

Summer

Bluegills

FALL

(From the first cooling trend down to the coldest water)

The onset of cooling water sets bluegills to wandering back and forth from shallows to deep water on a less-regular schedule. At this time of year it can often be difficult to predict where they will be found. As a general trend, though, as the temperature of the lake continues to drop, the fish will move to increasingly deeper water until they reach a depth of about fifteen feet.

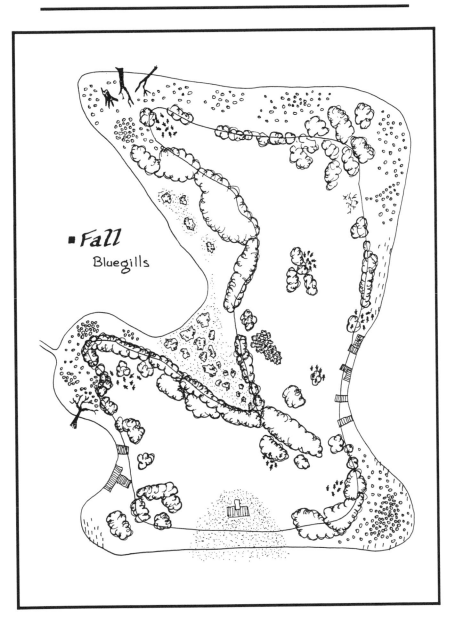

■ *Fall*
Bluegills

Pumpkinseeds

General Habits and Habitat: The lives and habits of these colorful sunfish are very similar to those of the bluegills. The major differences are that the pumpkinseeds do not grow to the size of bluegills, nor do they stay as deep. Even the largest of the pumpkinseeds will usually be found in relatively shallow water, which makes them accessible to shorebound anglers throughout much of the year. Nonetheless, pumpkinseeds feed far less on surface insects than do bluegills; more of their food, of nymphs and crustaceans, is taken off the bottom. Pumpkinseeds spawn at the same time and in the same habitat as do bluegills.

Because of the pumpkinseed's close similarity to the bluegill, I will not go into detail about their habits for each period. The information on the bluegill may be applied profitably to the pumpkinseed.

Pike and Pickerel

These gamefish are not related to the sunfishes. Pike and pickerel are both in the pike family, along with the muskellunge. Most anglers of warm-water lakes will run across the chain pickerel. It is extremely widespread across the continent, not only within its natural range, which extends down the entire Eastern Seaboard and across much of the South, but through its extensive introduction to warm-water lakes throughout the country. The northern pike, on the other hand, is found in few warm-water lakes, but its introduction to suitable areas as a control of panfish and "trash-fish" populations is becoming increasingly widespread.

Both fish are typically non-schooling. Individuals lie in ambush for prey and, following a short, sudden rush, grab it in well-toothed jaws. Both pike and pickerel are partial to weed beds. Neither species feeds nocturnally.

Besides spawning, neither pike nor pickerel show a great deal of seasonal variation in life history. Both species are as active in cold-water periods as in summer (sometimes more so). Rather than detailing each calendar period for these species, therefore, I'll more briefly describe their year.

NORTHERN PIKE

General Habits and Habitat: This is a cold-water fish. It naturally occurs in the oligotrophic lakes of the Canadian Shield and the mesotrophic lakes of the northern United States. However, like the smallmouth bass, it may be prevalent in many eutrophic lakes that have younger characteristics, and it is being regularly introduced into other warm-water lakes, as well. You may very well come in contact with at least a small pike. They typically eat other fish and frogs, but the large individuals of the North can handle baby ducks, muskrats, and other small hapless creatures that venture near.

Pike are active throughout the cold-water period and are regularly caught through the ice. Their metabolism slows slightly, but they are still active feeders. They spend this period in the weeds on the deeper flats.

Spawning takes place very soon after ice-out in water temperatures of as low as forty degrees to as high as about the midfifties. No nest is built. The fish mate in shallow weedy coves and river mouths, and the fertilized eggs are left to fall where they may. After mating, individuals filter back to the weed beds on the flats.

Because pike are naturally cold-water fish, summer temperatures are stressful to them and they will seek the coldest areas of a warm-water lake that hold good weeds. They may become extremely hard to catch until the cooling temperatures of fall increase their comfort again.

CHAIN PICKEREL

General Habits and Habitat: Chain pickerel are quite similar to northern pike except that they are much more comfortable in warm-water lakes; in fact, these are their natural habitat. Like pike, pickerel are solitary lurkers. They hang, dead still, among the weeds in shallow water and rush out at frogs and fish, typically yellow perch. They are excellent fighters and a thrill to play on light tackle. Unfortunately, many anglers consider them a nuisance, mainly because there are no national organizations offering money and prestige for their capture.

During the cold-water period, pickerel are as active as in summer and are regularly caught through the ice on shiners or jigs. As in summer, pickerel inhabit the edges of weed beds in water from the extreme shallows down to about ten or twelve feet.

Pickerel spawn very early in the year when the water temperature is between approximately forty-seven degrees and fifty-two degrees. Spawning in pickerel is similar to spawning in pike. After the eggs are scattered, individuals return to the shallow weed beds

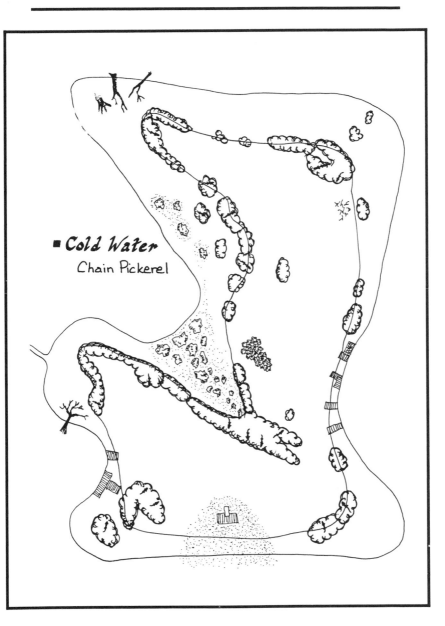

■ *Cold Water*
    Chain Pickerel

where they can be found throughout the rest of the year.

Pickerel are particularly exciting to fish by skittering a weedless lure over the tops of lily-pad patches during the summer period. In many warm-water lakes your chances are fifty-fifty as to whether a strike will come from a pickerel or a bass.

Other Species

There are three more species you should know about if you are going to haunt warm-water lakes. The yellow perch is a member of the perch family and is one of the most widespread and popular species found in fresh water. The white perch—unrelated to the yellow perch and actually not a perch at all but a member of the family of temperate basses to which also belongs the striped bass, among others—is a fish originally of eastern rivers, but that is now commonly landlocked and introduced throughout the country. The bullheads, of which there are actually three common species (black, brown, and yellow), are a family of catfishes that occur throughout the country. All of the above species are excellent panfish both as food and sport.

YELLOW PERCH

General Habits and Habitat: Whether jigged through the ice or nabbed on a hot summer day, these willing feeders are fun to catch year-round. Yellow perch are schooling fish that typically form enormous congregations of similarly sized fish.

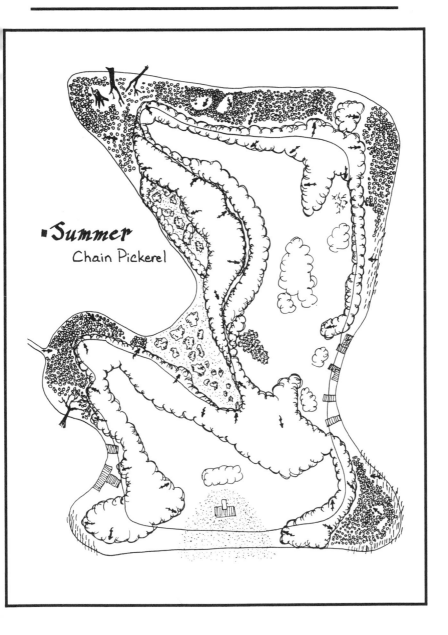

Summer

Chain Pickerel

Yellow perch are a remarkably adaptable species. They are typically the main forage in the oligotrophic lakes of the Far North, providing the principal menu item for northern pike. Yet they also thrive in the eutrophic lakes that are the subject of this book, providing forage for largemouth bass and chain pickerel. They are arguably the tastiest species in fresh water, as well as one of the most obliging biters. Anchored over a school of yellow perch, a youngster fishing bait or artificials can be kept interested for hours.

Yellow perch primarily eat small fish and the nymphs of aquatic insects, but they will also feed on crayfish and some plant material. Rarely do they take food off the surface, and they do not eat at night. At night, schools tend to migrate into shallow water, where the fish sleep on the bottom until daylight.

Usually, yellow perch spawn right after the pike and pickerel, when the water temperature is about fifty degrees. Individuals move into the weedy shallows, into river mouths, and up creeks where mating takes place. No nest is built, and the stringy, gelatinous masses of eggs are laid over vegetation where they develop without parental care. Each female may lay as many as 75,000 eggs. Thus, in warm-water lakes where sufficient predators exist, yellow perch provide the main forage and are kept in balance. Where the larger predators are lacking, the yellow perch population can quickly explode, crowding out other panfish species and producing a lake full of nothing but stunted perch.

During the spawning period, large individuals can easily be caught in the shallows. Once spawning is over, however, schools of similarly sized individuals regroup, and the schools with the biggest perch head for deep water. The schools of smaller fish usually stay in shallower water. All the schools relate to weeds and are bottom-oriented, but they travel, following the baitfish upon which they feed. Throughout the year, yellow perch tend to stay close to the bottom at whatever depth the particular school is occupying. Schools of small fish may be found over the tops of sunken islands and humps in only three feet of water. The schools of big fish, however, may be down as far as fifty feet in deep lakes. Generally, the largest fish will be near the bottom in the deepest water that is still well oxygenated and holds weeds. Most of the time, a school of yellow perch of one size or another will not take you long to locate.

WHITE PERCH

General Habits and Habitat: White perch occur naturally in a few rivers in the Northeast. There they are anadromous, living mainly in salt water and moving up the freshwater rivers and streams to spawn. However, there are many warm-water lakes in the East where naturally landlocked populations exist, and those have proven to be such excellent sport fisheries that white perch are increasingly being stocked in other sections of the country.

The white perch is not a perch. It is related to the striped bass, a member of the temperate basses family. Thus, white perch are related neither to yellow perch (which is a true perch) nor to the largemouth or smallmouth basses (which are sunfishes). The white perch is a schooling fish of open water. Its silvery coloration, devoid of any markings, shows it to be a fish that does not spend time among weeds either hunting or hiding, and that habit makes it entirely different from all the other species I have described. Schools of white perch travel the deeper (to about thirty feet), open waters of the lake, chasing schools of two- to three-inch baitfish or scouring the sandy bottoms for insect larvae. They will also take insects off the surface in open water.

White perch spawn in the shallows and up inflowing streams when the water temperature has climbed into the sixties. A female may lay as many as 150,000 eggs, which are left to develop on their own. Schools of young fish remain in shallow water while the schools of larger fish form out in the main part of the lake. During the post-spawn and summer periods, white perch feed mainly on small fish. During the fall, cold water, and pre-spawn periods, minnows of the right size are less available, and the schools concentrate more on insects and crustaceans.

Schools of white perch are often extremely hard to locate. Some days, dozens may be caught on live worms or small jigs in a particular spot, while on the next day they are nowhere to be found. Still, they provide such an excellent fight on light tackle and are so good to eat that white-perch devotees are among the most rabid of anglers.

I apologize for not being more helpful in locating white perch, but that is the nature of the beast; I know many avid white-perch anglers, some with years of experience, but none who can readily locate the schools. Me neither.

BULLHEADS

General Habits and Habitat: The yellow, black, and brown bullheads each differ slightly in appearance and preferred habitat, but they are similar enough to discuss in general terms. All are catfish and all lack scales. Their eyes are small and of far less use to them than their senses of smell and touch. The latter sense is largely aided by the whisker-like barbels that project from around their mouths.

Bullheads are strictly bottom-dwelling scavengers, eating whatever they find, dead or alive, animal or vegetable, on the bottoms of mucky warm-water lakes. But their appearance and habits belie their value as superb eating and excellent sport. A twelve-inch bullhead can fight like a good-size bass and give the angler quite a thrill. It is removing them from the hook that is the problem, because they croak and flap, spreading black slime on everything they touch and poking you in the hands with their painfully sharp lateral spines.

Bullheads, especially the black, are among the last survivors of eutrophic lakes in the last stages of lake life. They can withstand extremely high water temperatures and terribly depleted oxygen supplies.

Spawning takes place when the water temperature is well up near seventy degrees. A depression is dug in the bottom by both the male and female. Very few eggs are laid, usually only about five hundred, but the diligent care by both parents at first and then the male alone, results in extremely low mortality of the young.

Bullheads spend most of the year on the bottom in warm water, but they are still active throughout the cold-water period, if somewhat slowed down, and are sometimes caught through the ice. They are mainly nocturnal feeders and can find food in murky water as easily as in clear. Although not schooling fish per se, bullheads often congregate in prime areas of abundant food, so where you catch one, you are likely to catch others.

Although bullheads are often caught during the day, they are best caught at dusk and at night. Fish right on the bottom with live bait—a gob of nightcrawlers is perfect. They have been known to take lures, but that is definitely the hard way to do it.

SPECIES	FAVORED SPAWNING TEMPERATURES IN °F	NEST BUILT?
Largemouth Bass	62 to 65	yes
Smallmouth Bass	56 to 64	yes
Crappies	64 to 68	yes
Bluegills	60 and +	yes
Pumpkinseeds	60 and +	yes
Northern Pike	45 to 50	no
Chain Pickerel	47 to 52	no
Yellow Perch	45 to 50	no
White Perch	64 to 69	no
Bullheads	70 and +	yes

Okay, those are a few of the most widespread and popular species of warm-water lakes. Certainly there are others, and I hope I have not neglected one of your favorites. If I have, though, you can simply find out about its life history from another book or a biologist in your state's fisheries department, and then apply that information as needed.

Now that you know how most of the inhabitants of Lake Tepidaqua live and what they are doing throughout the year, it is finally time to put all your knowledge to work. Let's go fishing—at least on paper.

6

Analyzing the Data

USING YOUR EYES AND KNOWLEDGE

You now have a store of valuable knowledge about how fish live and what is important to them. You also have some useful tools that can help you evaluate a fishing situation, parts of which may not be easily observable.

If nothing else, you have your eyes. Those will help you determine not only a great deal of vital information about the condition of the light, but also a vast assortment of environmental details that, collectively, can make you a superb fisherman. Furnishing those eyes with a pair of polarized sunglasses will greatly augment their ability to see below the surface of the water, thereby increasing the amount of information they will provide.

Let's also assume that you have a sonar unit of some sort that will help you precisely locate underwater structure and topography. Such a device will most likely help you catch more fish, for it will allow you to find the precise places that you now know you want to find. A thermometer for measuring the surface temperature of the water will also prove useful, since much of a fish's behavior is temperature-related during some parts of its year. Nonetheless, those are not sufficient to make you a "better fisherman." To be a better fisherman, you must also learn how to use your powers of observation in concert with your knowledge.

I'm going to walk you through a few examples of how you might go about putting all these things together to form a plan for some outings. You may recall that it is the formation of a solid plan, based on the best possible observations and a background of reliable knowledge, that is your initial goal each time you go fishing. Fishing without a plan is a purely random activity that rarely results in anything but frustration.

Because most anglers who venture forth upon a warm-water lake are hoping to catch largemouth bass, I'll use that exemplary gamefish as an example. The thinking that follows, however, and the kinds of things you should always be looking for, apply equally to the pursuit of all warm-water fish.

So we're fishing Lake Tepidaqua in the middle of a lovely spring day. That, of course, could mean anything, depending on where on the continent your particular Lake Tepidaqua is located. But rather than alienate anyone, let's just say that the surface temperature of the water is sixty degrees where you've launched your boat near the beach.

Weed growth in the lake, at least from what you can see in the shallows, is still pretty sparse. The area in which you know there will be carpets of lily pads in the summer is showing only a few scattered leaves. As you scout the edges of the lake, you can see the occasional bright, platter-sized spot on the bottom that indicates the arrival into nesting areas of the first, eager, largemouth males.

The weather has been warm and sunny for the last three days, and the wind from the south has been strong at times. Now, though, the day is bright and nearly calm with only a few fair-weather cumulus clouds at the edges of the sky. The water in the lake is clear and barely ruffled. What's the plan?

To be perfectly honest, on exquisite spring days like the one described, my initial tendency is to sit back and become catatonic, barely able to form a single coherent thought, let alone formulate a plan. But for your sake, I will force myself, and my thinking would go like this: First, the bass are in the pre-spawn stage, but close to spawning. Their tendency, at least for the males, will be strongly toward the shallows. The big females, however, will still be hanging back toward deeper water, but definitely orienting toward potential spawning areas.

The days have been warm and sunny and the wind has been mixing the water well. Both for the higher temperatures and because of the spawning instinct, the shallows are the places to be. Because of the several days of warm south wind, I'll work the northern (windward) side of the lake. The bass should hit a lure willingly.

However, the sky is bright and the water is clear and relatively calm. The fish will be seeking cover from the ultraviolet rays while yet succumbing to the urge to move shallower. That makes any weeds in the windward shallows extremely important. It also makes any undercut banks and overhanging brush and vegetation prime bass locations.

My plan will be to cast first to the banks, working carefully to put my lure as close as possible to the edge, even to the point of letting it land on the bank or in the bushes, and coaxing it gently into the water, making it fall straight down and keeping it as long as possible in that near-bank area before retrieving it back to the boat. If nothing develops after a couple of dozen casts in prime spots, I'll move out toward deeper water until I find the first, thick, growth of weeds. I'll find them either by watching my sonar unit, seeing them through the clear water with the aid of my polarized sunglasses, or dragging a lure along the bottom until I feel them. Then I'll work those thoroughly. If still nothing happens, I'll move right out to the first dropoff and fish the edge.

As I move along the shallow flat in the back of the cove, though, I see the wake of a spooked fish. It's a bluegill, and he moved in my direction, not away. That means it was not I who scared him, but something farther back in the shallows under the bushes. I suspect my initial part of the plan is going to pay off right away. Even so, I still plan to move out to the edge for the big females after I've gotten my fill of the males under the bank.

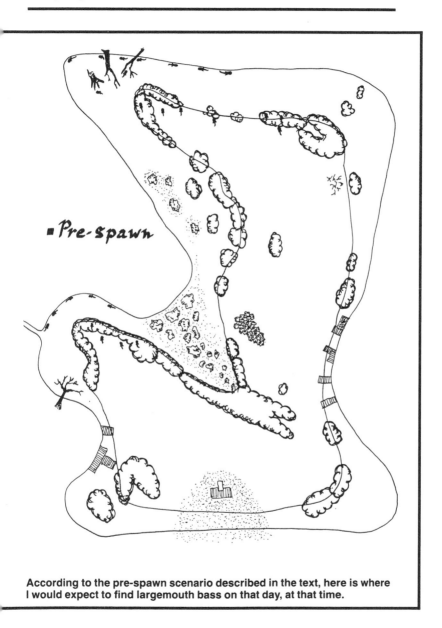

According to the pre-spawn scenario described in the text, here is where I would expect to find largemouth bass on that day, at that time.

Okay, now it is summer. I don't care where your Lake Tepidaqua is, because there is nothing you can call this but summer: The air temperature has been in the high eighties for the past week. The water temperature is eighty degrees. For the last few days the humidity has been comfortable, but the sky has been bright; letting bare skin come in contact with an aluminum boat seat has been both a startling and woeful experience. There has been some wind. Today, though, it looks like it may rain later in the afternoon. The sky is generally gray, and it is very hot, extremely muggy, and dead calm. Weed growth in the lake is at its peak and has been for a month. What's the plan?

Well, there's no doubt that the bass are in their summer period, which is generally quite stable. They do not move around much and will be pretty well settled into the best food and cover areas between the shallows and the twelve-foot depth on the flats. Those shallows areas will be the ones with the thickest and densest cover of surface weeds.

It has been clear and comfortable for the past week, so the ultraviolet rays will not have been mitigated much by moisture in the air. Today, though, it is actually cloudy. My guess would be that the bass will be more active and more likely to come up out of the weeds to hit a lively lure. I'm going to start on the flats where the bottom is about eight feet deep and the weeds are growing to within a few feet of the surface (I can see them by just looking over the side of the boat). I'm going to use a lure that has a good, enticing wounded-minnow action, diving to just within the tops of the weeds, and that will suspend there or rise extremely slowly when I stop reeling. I'm going to look especially

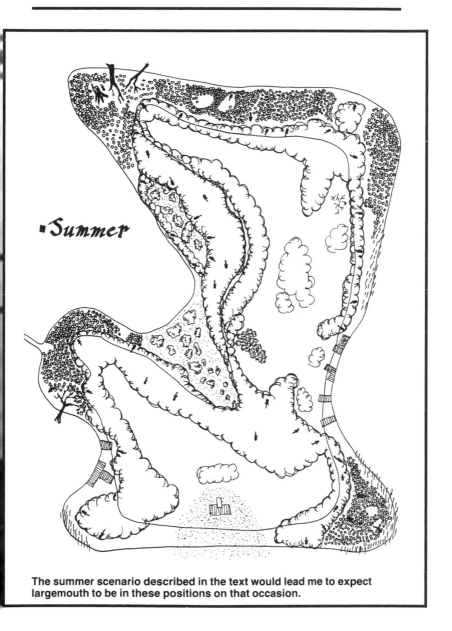

Summer

The summer scenario described in the text would lead me to expect largemouth to be in these positions on that occasion.

for edges, whether in the form of the actual edge of the weed bed at that depth or the edge where one type of weed meets another (again at that depth). If I'm unsuccessful, I'll move a little shallower, seeking the *inside* edges of the weeds in water from six to three feet deep. My thinking is simply that the reduction in ultraviolet rays by the overcast will set the bass on a search for the abundant young fish in the shallower, more open water between the submerged beds and the shoreline.

I'll also try skittering a weedless lure over the carpet of lily pads in the shallows. I can hear the kissing sound of bass hitting dragonflies coming from those areas and have actually seen a few large splashes coming from open spots among the pads. In those spots where the pads suddenly stop because of deep water, I'll try that wounded-minnow lure again, too. If the wind stays down, I'll also try dropping a bug among the pads with my fly rod. That may prove the most fun of all; with this cloud cover, the bass should not be reluctant to come to the surface.

Next, we've got a water temperature of sixty degrees again, but this time the days are getting shorter. Weed beds are thinning out and the nights are noticeably cooler. It has been raining for two days, a cold steady rain that has rather quickly caused the water temperature to drop several degrees. Today, though, it is finally sunny. The clouds cleared out spectacularly, and the sky is as blue as a jay. A sharp, fresh breeze is blowing from the northwest. What's the plan?

Simple. The cold front will have sent the bass into heavy cover or deep water. With the cover thinning and the cold-water period approaching, the tendency of the

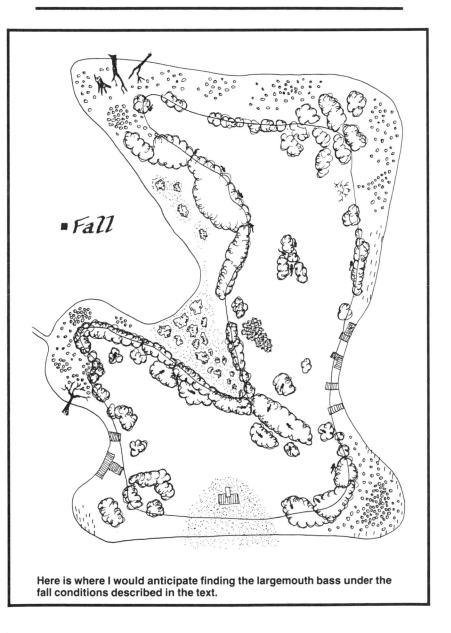

■ *Fall*

Here is where I would anticipate finding the largemouth bass under the fall conditions described in the text.

bass is to go deep anyway. The cold rain will have certainly made the shallows inhospitable, but the strong sun today may, by later in the afternoon, warm them sufficiently to attract a few wandering fish. Still, the best bet is to fish the deeper points and dropoffs with something slow, tempting, and easy to catch. Surface lures are definitely out. On my usual Lake Tepidaqua, I'm well acquainted with the locations of the points, sunken islands, and dropoffs from the flats. If I were on an unknown Lake Tepidaqua, I would first look at the surrounding landscape to get my clues to where points may extend into the lake and where the banks may drop off steeply. Then I'd check those spots out with my sonar unit to find the places to begin executing my plan for today.

These three examples show how you can quickly formulate a workable plan for any day of fishing: You observe the current situation, apply it to what you have learned about the fish you are after, and then you search for that precise part of the fish's environment in which your thinking has led you to believe the fish should be. Once you have made a plan, stick to it unless something strongly urges you to adopt another. Most anglers—and now I'm talking about the ones who know how to think about fishing, not the ones whose understanding extends only as far as the insight to fish where there is water—are too impatient to give their plans a proper workout. Even being in the right place with the right lure does not guarantee nonstop success most of the time. Having the confidence in your thinking to thoroughly and patiently follow your plan is what catches fish.

❧ On the other hand, if you have analyzed the situation and determined that you should be fishing the weeds in the extreme shallows, but you notice that another angler has been pulling up one ten-pound bass after another while anchored over fifteen feet of water off a rocky point, by all means go ahead and fish some deep rocky points. Being adaptable catches fish, too. To that point let me add another few words of advice: Always keep your eyes open for potential fish-producing circumstances. Any time you are cruising around the lake, single-mindedly executing your day's plan, be sure not to be *too* single-minded. Learn to spot locations and situations that point to a big-fish possibility even though they may be inconsistent with your plan. Fish, after all, are not machines; factors beyond our understanding or perception may move them to be in places we did not anticipate finding them.

Watch not only for significant edges but for other subtle signs as well. An area of particularly abundant insect life should set your nostrils twitching. So should a particular profusion of frogs or wading birds. All of those signs indicate an area especially rich in bass food (the wading birds share the bass's appetite for baitfish and frogs) where you should at least focus your eyes and make a few exploratory casts. Watch, too, for any movement of the water, and never fail to cast to swirls. You never know if the disturbance was caused by a bluegill chasing minnows or a ten-pound bass chasing bluegills. Either way, the commotion indicates current feeding activity and the presence of bass food.

At any rate, the concept of having a workable plan to follow is something I cannot stress enough, even if you think I already *have* stressed it enough. The three examples I gave of how to go about it may prove to produce few fish. I may have failed to take into account some consideration that makes my plan less effective than someone else's. Nonetheless, having even an imperfect plan is better than no plan at all. It is somewhat like the old gag about the stopped watch being better than one that is always fast: At least the stopped one is right twice a day. You can learn from even a faulty plan; you gain nothing from random bustle.

You have undoubtedly noticed that while I have explained in this chapter how to think about *where* to fish, I have been entirely vague about what to fish *with*, offering only a few indefinite references to using "a lure that has a good, enticing wounded-minnow action" and "something slow, tempting, and easy to catch." That is not purely out of perversity and the fear that you will one day show up at my favorite fishing spot and show me up. In the next chapter, I will, in fact, offer some solid advice on the best tools available for converting your plans into landed fish.

7

The Tools for the Job

LURES YOU SHOULD HAVE

There is no question that most fishing lures are designed not so much to catch fish as to catch fishermen. The only way to survive in the fishing department of any of the large discount stores is to know what you want to buy and not be drawn by any of the other millions of items. And, for god's sake, never ask the opinion of a clerk; ten times out of ten (in my experience), he has never fished in his life and was in fact working in the housewares department until yesterday.

It is not that the majority of lures are worthless—most, in fact, will eventually catch fish—but that they are redundant. By thinking of different types of fishing lures as tools having different characteristics that make them appropriate for solving distinct problems, you can avoid loading yourself down with a lot of superfluous stuff and buying ten different lures that are all designed to do essentially the same job.

157

The best way to go about provisioning your tackle box is to consider the habits and habitats of the various fish you are trying to catch. Basically, you will often be fishing in weeds, sometimes right down in them, but also in open water along their edges or over their tops. You will, on various occasions, want to fish on the water's surface, on the lake's bottom, and at various but precise depths in between. You will want lures that are designed to be effective when retrieved fast and some that can be retrieved extremely slowly without making obvious their artificiality or losing their allure. That sounds like a lot, but you can be reasonably well prepared for all those eventualities with surprisingly few lures.

Any lure may come in a variety of sizes. Generally, you will want to choose sizes appropriate to the types of fish you wish to catch. Sunnies, for example, have small mouths and usually eat small prey: Lures for sunnies should, therefore, be quite small. Crappies are very particular about the size of the minnows they chase: Lures between one and a half and two and a half inches in length are appropriate for crappies. Bass and pickerel will hit much larger lures, including plastic worms eight inches or longer, but they will take smaller lures, too.

Having an assortment of lure sizes allows you to catch a variety of species, but you must always keep in mind that your tackle must be balanced. Heavy bait-casting rods with seventeen-pound line will not cast $\frac{1}{16}$-ounce lures. For those, you need ultralight spinning tackle spooled with two- or four-pound test. All decent rods are stamped with the range of lure and line weights for which they are designed. Ignoring that information inevitably yields the same results as does the serious misuse of any tool.

And not only is an assortment of rods and reels useful for handling different types of fish, but a variety of bait-casting, spinning, and fly tackle is valuable, too, for handling a variety of situations. There is no tackle better than a good bait-casting outfit for winching big bass out of heavy cover. Likewise, light spinning tackle is wonderfully accommodating for working a variety of lure types in relatively open water. And nothing beats fly tackle for presenting surface bugs upon the glassy surface of a pond, whether for big bass or feisty bluegills. Although each type of tackle is extremely versatile and can be used in most situations, each has its particular métier in which it is unsurpassed. Learn to use all three types of tackle.

Lure color can be a real can of worms. Depending upon the time of day, quality of light, clarity of water, amount of weeds, bottom composition, and whims of the fish, the color of a lure may be of little consequence or great import. To complicate matters, lure manufacturers have made available every possible color and finish you can imagine.

To greatly simplify color choices, I use this general rule of thumb: For surface lures, a white or yellow bottom is all that is important (black for night fishing); the fish never see the top. For crankbaits: silver, gold, chartreuse, and anything that actually imitates the colors and markings of genuine forage in the lake. For soft-plastic worms, tubes, and grubs: a selection of white or sand, black or violet, brown or orange, and chartreuse. Try bright colors on bright days, darker colors on darker days, and black at night. That is the most simplified selection that is reasonable. Beyond that, buy anything that your budget allows or your propensity for collecting demands. Now to the actual lures.

Soft-Bodied Grubs

This lure, in a variety of sizes, is undoubtedly the most versatile proven fish-catcher you can find. Although not weedless, it can be fished at a variety of depths and will catch nearly every species in most situations.

Soft-bodied grub rigged on a lead-head jig.

The grub itself is merely a grub-shaped piece of soft plastic with, usually, one or two wiggly tails that provide a sinuous action when moved through the water. The grub must be threaded on a jig head, which is a hook with a piece of lead molded on near the eye. Jig heads come in a variety of weights and sizes, typically from $\frac{1}{32}$ to $\frac{1}{4}$ of an ounce. The grubs are available in sizes from one inch to four inches. You can buy bags of the grubs and jigs separately and in quantity. Mister Twister is one popular and dependable brand.

In the smallest sizes, grubs will reliably catch all the panfish, except bullheads. In the larger sizes, they are readily accepted by the basses, pickerel, and pike.

The natural tendency of this lure is to sink, of course, but the rate at which it does so can be varied by the relative jig/grub combination. A smaller grub with a heavy jig will sink like a stone, while a large grub and lighter jig will tend to drift more casually to the bottom. Depending on that combination and the speed and technique of your retrieve, you can use this lure in a wide variety of circumstances.

The lure's most effective use under most conditions is to be cast into the area you want to fish, allowed to fall entirely to the bottom, and then hopped back to you at moderate speed by sharp twitching of the rod tip vertically while you continue to reel slowly.

Soft-bodied jigs in sizes from $\frac{1}{32}$ of an ounce to $\frac{1}{8}$ of an ounce, and used with ultralight spinning tackle, are perfect for sunnies, bluegills, crappies, and yellow perch. They are also a good choice for bass in the fall when they begin to downsize their forage.

OTHER JIGS

There are also jigs of various sizes that come in other forms. Some are close relatives of the soft-bodied grub, but come already rigged. Where the previously discussed grub-and-jig are often generic, these similar variations can be found under such names as "Road Runner," "Stump Jumper," "Foxee Jigs," "Fuzz-E-Grubs," and a million others.

There are also small jigs known generically as crappie jigs that are made from marabou feathers tied to a jig head. Those, too, are wonderfully versatile and can catch anything from sunnies to pike.

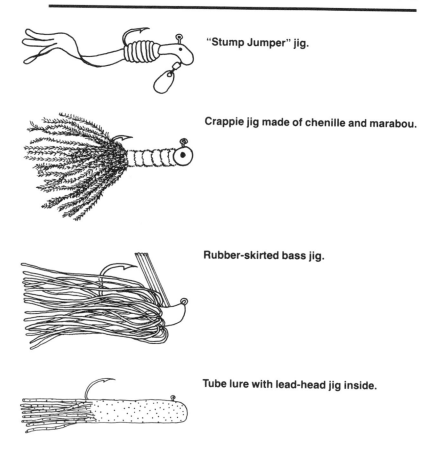

"Stump Jumper" jig.

Crappie jig made of chenille and marabou.

Rubber-skirted bass jig.

Tube lure with lead-head jig inside.

Larger jigs with live-rubber skirts are available for bass. They are often made more attractive by the attachment of a pork rind or synthetic trailer. They are a good choice for working close to the banks during pre-spawn.

Tube lures, which are basically tubular grubs in which the lead head of the jig is inserted and hidden, are a relatively new and very effective variation.

All these jigs are extremely useful and highly adaptable for all species.

Plastic Worms

Soft-plastic worms come in a range of sizes from about four inches to as long as ten, although six to seven and a half inches is the most common length. They are typically rigged Texas-style, which means that a worm hook is inserted into the head for about a quarter of an inch, brought out the side again, then turned 180 degrees and reinserted farther down the body so that the point is buried in the plastic. This arrangement makes the worm entirely weedless, yet if a fish hits it, the hook can easily be yanked through the worm and into the fish's jaw.

Plastic worm showing Texas-rigging and bullet weight.

Used without any additional weight, this lure can be skittered across mats of floating weeds. Weighted, it can be enticingly crawled along the bottom and retrieved through thick cover. It is one of the most effective bass lures ever developed, but is generally limited to that genus.

Texas-rigged worms are my choice when fish are hunkered down in weed beds, as during cold fronts.

Spinnerbaits

This is another lure generally intended for the larger species—basses, pickerel, and pike—but in the smallest sizes may be appropriate for crappies, as well.

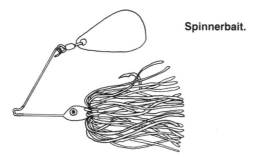

Spinnerbait.

These are excellent lures for prospecting weed beds, for their design allows them to move through heavy cover without hanging up and collecting greenery. They can be worked close to the surface or allowed to fall to any depth. They can therefore be used much like jigs, or steadily retrieved to trigger impulse-strikes.

Good pre-spawn, post-spawn, and fall lures, spinnerbaits are perfect for searching when fish are spread out and on the move.

Crankbaits

These are usually wood or plastic fish-shaped lures with underhanging lips. Most often they float at rest and wobble down to a specific depth when retrieved.

They come in every size and depth-design and can be used for bass, pickerel, pike, yellow perch, and crappie. Even sunnies and bluegills will occasionally hit a small crankbait. The size and position of the lip determines at what depth a crankbait will run. You should have some that run extremely shallow (one to three feet), at mid-depth (four to eight feet), and deep (ten to twenty feet). That may actually involve more than just three lures; the depths I just suggested are not specific to the lures, but to the lake. At any rate, crankbaits afford you the unique opportunity to create a system for fishing at predetermined depths with reasonable assurance that that is actually where your lure is.

Crankbait.

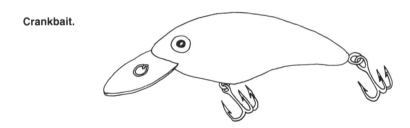

Crankbaits are perfect for covering points and dropoff edges, working the tops and edges of weed beds, and for carefully exploring specific depths when your sonar unit tells you that is where the fish are suspending. They are never particularly weedless, however, and quickly lose their action when they pick up vegetation.

Surface Lures

These are lures that are meant to be worked right on top of the water. They come in an extraordinary variety of sizes and styles and can be used for just about any species that will feed at the surface.

Most surface lures incorporate some device for creating a disturbance: propellers, cupped faces that pop against the water, appendages that create splashy movement, and so on. Others, though, are quiet, often imitating frogs or badly crippled minnows. Those meant to be worked in dense cover are relatively weedless; others are not and should be used not actually *in* the surface weeds but *near* them.

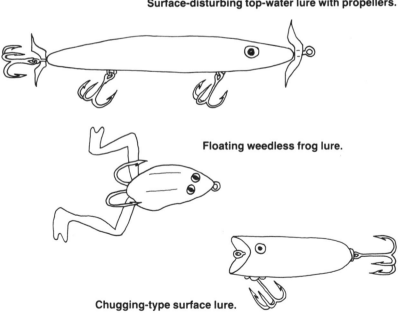

Surface-disturbing top-water lure with propellers.

Floating weedless frog lure.

Chugging-type surface lure.

The usual technique is to cast a surface lure out, let it sit absolutely still until the rings of disturbance dissipate, and then move it ever so slightly (a foot or less), allowing it to sit some more. There are times, however, when the situation demands that the lure be burned across the surface, but always try the quiet approach first.

Surface lures work best on calm days. Try them near lily pads on overcast days or near dawn and dusk, when fish will not be reluctant to approach the surface because of harsh ultraviolet rays.

Flies and Bugs

These are lures that must be cast with a fly rod. For panfish, they are my absolute first choice. Surface flies like tiny poppers and foam spiders will catch bluegills and sunfish on most days. When those species will not come to the surface, small Woolly Buggers, wet flies used for trout, and many other subsurface creations will catch yellow perch, crappies, sunnies, and bluegills.

Deer-hair bass bug for use with a fly rod.

For bass, pickerel, and pike, larger flies, both on the surface and under, work extremely well. When bass are hitting surface lures, I always prefer deer-hair or cork poppers. If you have never learned to cast with a fly rod, warm-water species are the ones to practice on. They are usually forgiving of sloppy casts, unlike trout, and will often hit flies when no other lure will do.

Others

Make no mistake, the above lures are not the only ones in my tackle box, but they are the ones I find myself using most often to solve the problems of catching fish. Once I've analyzed the situation and devised my plan for the day, one of those lures is likely to be just the ticket for fishing most effectively where I think the fish are to be found.

There are a couple of others I can recommend, though. Spoons, like the Dardevle, are particularly appealing to pickerel and pike. They do, however, tend to become infuriating to use in weeds.

Dardevle spoon.

The Johnson Silver Minnow, on the other hand, especially when attached to a pork-rind frog, is an exceptional lure for bass, pike, and pickerel in even the thickest mess of cover. Skittered over the tops of lily-pad patches, this combination regularly results in sudden explosions right up through the leaves. Another good lure for this is the Moss Boss, which requires no additional trailer.

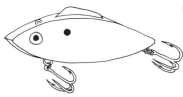

Johnson Silver Minnow (a weedless spoon) with a pork- frog trailer.

Ultrasonic vibrators, or Rat-L-Trap-type lures, are good things to have in your tackle box. They are vertically flattened minnow-shaped lures loaded with rattling BBs. They cast like bullets and sink fairly quickly, but otherwise function like a cross between a crankbait and a jig. These are good for exploring points, humps, rock piles, channels, and other structure.

Ultrasonic vibrator, or Rat-L-Trap type lure.

Live Bait

I am not an avid user of live bait, but there is no question that there are times when nothing will get a fish to bite like a juicy worm, a nervous cricket, or a panicked shiner. The cold-water period for bass just about demands live bait for decent results. Bullheads will rarely hit lures or flies, but a wriggling wad of nightcrawlers is seldom rejected.

Young children rarely have the coordination to cast lures, making live bait the preferred way of getting them excited about fishing. A #10 or #12 hook baited with a piece of worm and suspended about eighteen

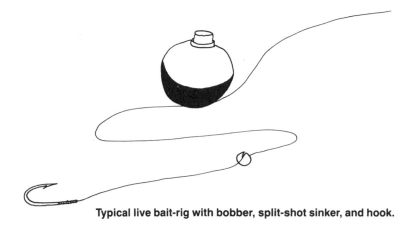

Typical live bait-rig with bobber, split-shot sinker, and hook.

inches under a bobber will keep even the most jaded youngster interested for a couple of hours.

Worms, minnows, frogs, crayfish, crickets, leeches, grubs, and hellgrammites are the most common live baits sold in bait shops. Generally, being alive, they provide their own action and do not, as do lures, necessitate constant casting and retrieving to give them motion. But they must still be fished in the locations and at the depths at which your analysis of the situation determines the fish to be. Don't expect the fish to come rushing in from great distances just because you have lowered some natural food into the water. Everything in this book applies as much to the use of live bait as to artificials.

Beyond those basic suggestions, I urge you to get yourself a copy of a good tackle catalog like the one put out by Bass Pro Shops of Springfield, Missouri: 1(800)227–7776. It is encyclopedic in its listings and descriptions of lures and tackle. Peruse it and read the descriptions of the lures. Much of that, of course, is hype provided by the manufacturers, and the claims of fish-catching proficiency are to be taken with even less than a grain of salt. But you can get a pretty good idea of what each lure is designed to do and, just as you would appraise a catalog from Craftsman, Stanley, Makita, or Rockwell, decide for yourself which tools you will likely need to best solve the problems you will encounter.

Afterword

CATCHING FISH

If you have absorbed the information in this book, you will now at least have a clue that there is more to successful fishing than the random presentation of bait. Whether you can actually apply the information toward developing successful game plans will be a function of how well I've communicated the information, how well you've ingested it, how much you care about improving your fishing, how much opportunity you get to practice, how well you learn from experience, and whether you have remembered to turn around three times and spit on your lure.

Seriously though, the intelligent application of the material herein will help you catch more fish, and therein lies the irony of my profession. As a fishing writer, I am entrusted with the task of helping you become a more successful angler, but if I succeed, I become responsible for the ultimate decline of the sport. The greater number of successful anglers I create, the more pressure on the resource results. That is, unless I can also instill in you the importance of your responsibility not to abuse that resource.

Things are not as they used to be. We have learned from innumerable unlucky species that were once greatly abundant that we cannot mindlessly kill fish without adversely affecting the fishing. You, alone, are not likely to have much impact on any body of water but, collectively, several proficient anglers can make a noticeable difference over time.

It behooves you, as one who takes pleasure from the resource, to protect it by practicing catch-and-release. That means handling fish gently and as little as possible and returning them to the water carefully and promptly.

I do not advocate never killing a fish. All panfish make delicious eating and the harvesting of such fish may often actually improve some lakes in which the overpopulation of certain prey species is stunting the growth of its individuals. Gamefish are also good to eat, but large predators are a precious commodity. Their presence in a body of water makes that lake all the more exciting to fish, just from your knowing that the possibility of catching a big fish exists. The ability to grow large also represents genetic traits that must be allowed to endure. Particularly large individuals must be permitted to continue breeding for as long as possible. Female bass average about five thousand eggs per pound of body weight each year.

No one is asking you to abstain from keeping the occasional fish for food. But please do consider that a photograph may be as satisfactory a trophy as a dead fish, and that the better an angler you become, the more heartache you will suffer when there is nothing left to catch.

That said, I hope your fishing success now becomes as much improved as I fully expect it will.

Index